SMALL SIDED GAMES IN FOOTBALL

57 TRAINING ACTIVITIES

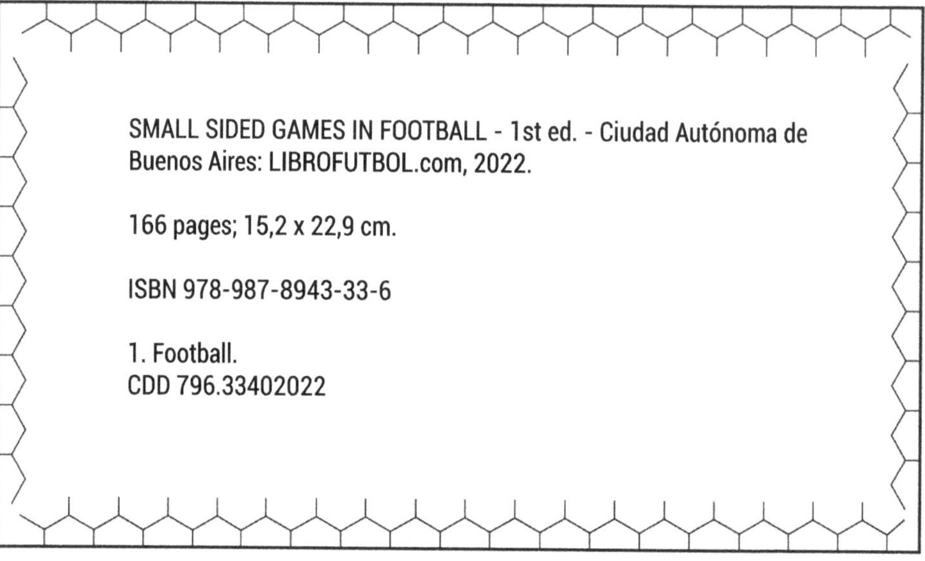

SMALL SIDED GAMES IN FOOTBALL - 1st ed. - Ciudad Autónoma de Buenos Aires: LIBROFUTBOL.com, 2022.

166 pages; 15,2 x 22,9 cm.

ISBN 978-987-8943-33-6

1. Football.
CDD 796.33402022

SMALL SIDED GAMES IN FOOTBALL

Cover: Luciano Medvetkin	Cover photo: © Alamy Ltd.
© 2022 – LIBROFUTBOL.com	All rights reserved

ISBN 978-987-8370-69-9	1st edition: November 2022

ediciones@librofutbol.com

+54 9 11 2215 1982

librofutbol

Av. Libertador 6898 - Núñez - City of Buenos Aires - Argentina

INDEX

PROLOGUE

Modern football is moving more and more towards "integrated" models of physical preparation. This term describes how activities without the ball are being abandoned more and more, with more prominence being given to activities that seek both the development of the physical parameters and, at the same time, the technical-tactical aspects of the game.

With this in mind, so-called "Small-Sided Games" are becoming increasingly common in weekly training plans. That is to say: games in reduced spaces with a variable number of players and specific rules designed to make the activity useful from a physical, technical, and tactical point of view.

This type of activity allows the player to train aerobic power from the physical-conditional point of view. However, with the introduction of the ball and the technical-tactical aspects of the game, it's also possible to stimulate the motivation of the athletes, leading them to apply maximum effort while feeling less fatigue, and with less perception of their work load.

Small-Sided Games are carried out within a limited playing area to simultaneously improve the physical and technical preparation of the players, optimizing training time and developing tactical knowledge. These games use different number of players and vary the dimensions of the playing area, the number of touches, and the duration of the activity, among other factors, to train various objectives. Small-sided games also allow the coach to vary the intensity of the training session.

A typical starting point for a game in small spaces would be one that includes the development of a two versus two, a situation that has been shown to induce a higher percentage, in respect to the player's maximum heart rate, than occurs in a three versus three or a four versus four situation. In addition, compared to three versus three or four versus four, the number of touches on the ball, dribbling actions, completed passes (the number of missed passes decreases), and shots on goal are all increased.

These results are the product of the analysis of the "Effects of Exercise Duration and Number of Players in Earth Rate Responses and Technical Skills During Futsal Small-Sided Games", and have been obtained through a scientific study of small-sided games played for four minutes, which is the standard minimum duration for these type of activities.

This study, along with many others, allows us to understand that by varying the dimensions of the field, the number of players, the presence or absence of a goalkeeper, the number of touches, and the duration of the activity, it is possible to influence the conditional aspects (heart rate, blood lactate), the technical conditions (number of passes, touches on the ball, tackles, finishes on goal, and dribbles) and other important aspects of football.

In conclusion, we can affirm that the use of small-sided games is definitely a very useful method for training both the conditional aspects (especially aerobic power) and technical-tactical aspects of the game. This allows the coach to make better use of their training time, a commodity that is often in short supply.

Results of some studies comparing the RPE (Rating of Perceived Exertion; Ratio of Perceived Effort) of a Small-Sided Game and an exercise without the ball have shown that the RPE of a SSG is lower. This confirms that there is a lower perception of tiredness in relation to the production of lactate in the blood, consistent with aerobic power work.

Through Small-Sided Games, it's possible for the player to give maximum effort without perceiving it, thanks to the presence of the ball and the objective of scoring a goal or winning the game. It influences the psychological and motivational aspects of the player, which should never be underestimated when talking about aerobic tasks.

Giorgio Polin
Coach
AS Cittadella

INTRODUCTION

Small-Sided Games (SSG) are technical activities presented in the form of games that are opportunely modified by the coach, based on the training context of the sport being practiced.

Therefore, these are typically activities that include modifications to the playing environment, the parameters of the task, the rules of the game, and above all, the number of participants, with the objective of recreating intense situations of cognitive, technical, and tactical effort that are very close to the performance model and the game itself.

Positive aspects: Numerous scientific studies have shown the usefulness of these types of tasks that allow, when adapted correctly, a 100% recreation of the situations found in competition, whether at the level of cognitive or physical load. From the technical-tactical point of view, it creates a series of opportunities to learn and resolve the most commonly occurring game situations. There is the possibility of carrying out these activities with either a reduced number of players or with the whole team (alternating the players who participate). In addition, SSGs can also be performed while increasing the level of difficulty, which makes them a means of training to improve technique: any technical errors and their consequent stoppages of play can be reduced thanks to the immediate re-insertion of the ball by the coach, a teammate, or a neutral player.

Negative aspects: like all activities, SSGs have a series of unfavorable points. The most difficult aspect to control is the effort: only a maximum effort from the players makes it possible to reach an intensity level similar to match play. As coaches, it is our job to find the right formula (with a team tournament, for example) that will allow the players to be 100% engaged. Another aspect that must be kept under control is energy expenditure: performed at high intensity, these tasks represent a great expenditure of energy that reaches levels of HR (heart rate) and VO2max (maximum oxygen consumption) close to and sometimes higher than 90 % of maximum level. It is essential to distribute the work and recovery times effectively, so as not to create situations of stress or injury.

Mode of execution: it has been scientifically proven how some parameters, such as the reduced number of players (from one versus one to three versus three), small fields, activities performed without a goalkeeper (with small goals), touch limits, and encouragement by the technical staff, can lead to an increase in the intensity of work during activities. It has been shown that the continuous method (a series of one repetition of medium- to -long duration) involves more specific work from the physical point of view, while intermittent work (more medium-to-short repetitions with recovery in between) is more useful from the point of view of learning and technical-tactical improvement.

Leopoldo Biasio
Bachelor of Sports Science
UEFA B License Coach

3 VERSUS 2 SUPERIORITY WITH A TEAMMATE IN SUPPORT

01

OPERATING METHOD Small-sided game

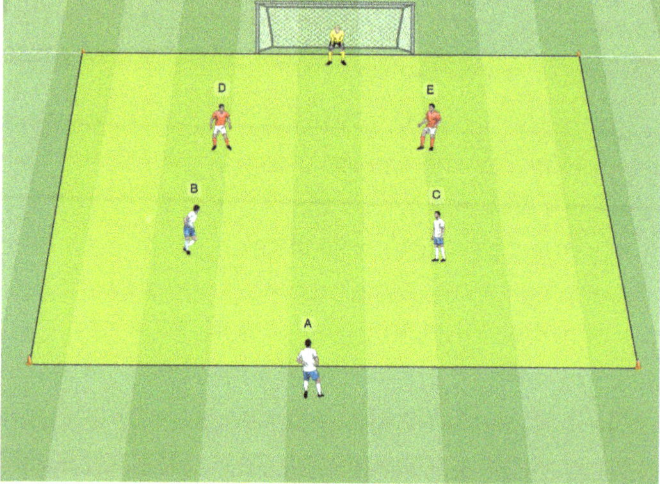

DURATION

24 minutes

OBJECTIVES

- **Possession**
- **Width**
- **Oriented control**
- **Defensive cover**

EQUIPMENT

- **Four cones**
- **Two bibs**
- **One goal**
- **Balls**

PREPARATION

Playing area: 20-25 x 25-30 meters.
Players: 5 + a goalkeeper.
Number of series: Four of 4 minutes with 2 minutes of recuperation between each series.

ORGANIZATION

In the space chosen for the activity use cones to mark out the playing area. Center a goal on one of the end lines. Divide the players into two teams; one team of three and another team of two, in bibs. The goalkeeper occupies the goal. One of the players from the team in superiority is positioned outside of the playing area, on the end line opposite the goal. Play starts with the goalkeeper, who passes across to the attacker who is outside the playing area.

RULES

- The team in numerical superiority attempts to score on the goal.
- The team in numerical inferiority tries to recover the ball and pass to their goalkeeper.
- Every ball recovered by the defenders and passed to the goalkeeper earns one point.
- After a goal is scored or the defenders earn a point, restart play by having the goalkeeper throw the ball to the attacker who is outside the playing area.
- The player from the team in numerical superiority who passes to the supporting player outside the playing area must exchange positions with them.
- When receiving the ball, the supporting player enters the field with an oriented control.

A possible passage of play: after passing to a teammate, the exterior player overlaps and tries to get free to receive a pass and shoot on goal.

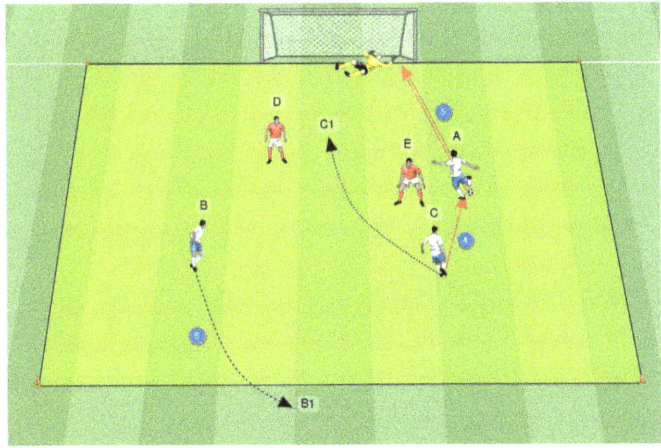

VARIATIONS

1. A goal is only valid after the team in numerical superiority carries out a combination of actions as determined by the coach:

   - Wall pass
   - Overlap
   - Cut
   - Pass
   - Dribbling
   - Aerial pass

2. Limit all players to three touches.

3. Limit the team in numerical superiority to three touches.

COACHING POINTS	<ul><li>In possession:<ul><li>Allow the players the freedom to take opponents on 1 versus 1.</li><li>The players rotate positions after every series.</li></ul></li><li>Out of possession:<ul><li>Demand high pressure in order to recover the ball as quickly as possible.</li><li>Balanced defending of the goal, according to collective tactical principles.</li><li>Players prepared for an attacking transition.</li><li>The goalkeeper gives verbal instructions to the defenders.</li></ul></li></ul>

3 VERSUS 2 + 2 EXTERNAL NEUTRALS

02

OPERATING METHOD Small-sided game

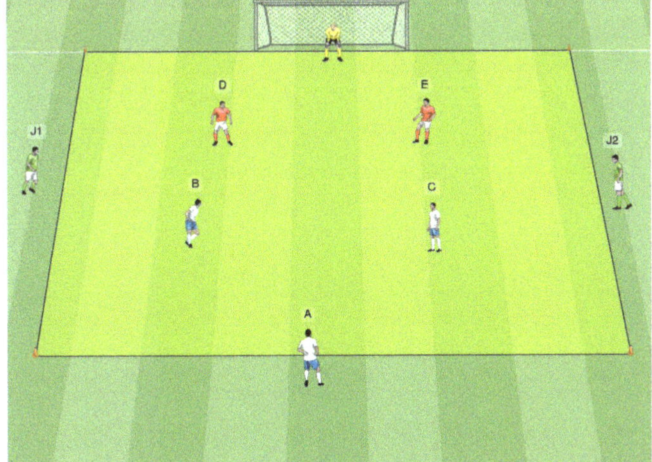

DURATION

24 minutes

OBJECTIVES

- **Possession**
- **Width**
- **Defensive cover**
- **Passing**

EQUIPMENT

- **Four cones**
- **Four bibs (two of one color and two of another)**
- **One goal**
- **Balls**

PREPARATION

Playing area: 20-25 x 25-30 meters.
Players: 7 + a goalkeeper.
Number of series: Four of 4 minutes with 2 minutes of recuperation between each series.

ORGANIZATION

In the space chosen for the activity use cones to mark out the playing area. Center a goal on one of the end lines. Divide the players into two teams; one team of three and another team of two, who wear bibs. The goalkeeper occupies the goal. One of the players from the team in numerical superiority is positioned outside of the playing area, on the end line opposite the goal. There are two neutral players positioned outside the playing area; one on each side. The goalkeeper initiates play by passing across to the player outside the playing area.

RULES

- The neutrals play with the team in possession.
- The team in numerical superiority attempts to score on the goal.
- The team in numerical inferiority scores points by crossing the end line across from the goal.
- After a goal is scored or the defenders earn a point, the goalkeeper restarts play by throwing the ball to the attacker who is outside the playing area.
- A goal may be scored after the team in numerical superiority carries out a combination as determined by the coach: wall pass, overlap, cut, pass, dribbling, or aerial pass.
- The interior players may not use the exterior players to carry out an overlap.

A possible passage of play: after passing to a teammate, the exterior attacking player overlaps and tries to get free to receive a pass and shoot on goal.

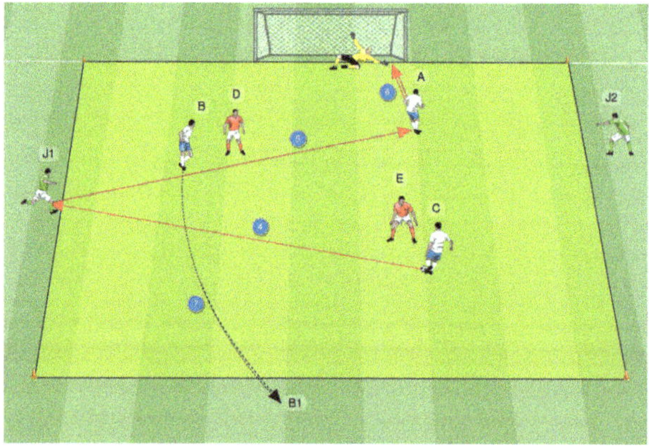

VARIATIONS

1. Limit all players to three touches.

2. Limit the team in numerical superiority to three touches.

3. The players can use the external neutral players to carry out an overlap.

COACHING POINTS	- In possession:
	  - This activity imposes a medium-to-high rhythm of play, training conditional capacities such as specific resistance.
	  - Allow the players freedom of action.
	  - Players rotate positions after every series.
	- Out of possession:
	  - Demand high pressure in order to recover the ball as quickly as possible.
	  - Balanced defending of the goal, according to collective tactical principles.
	  - Players prepared for an attacking transition.
	  - The goalkeeper gives verbal instructions to the defenders, and also takes up good positions in goal.

3 VERSUS 3 + 1 NEUTRAL IN SUPPORT

03

OPERATING METHOD Small-sided game

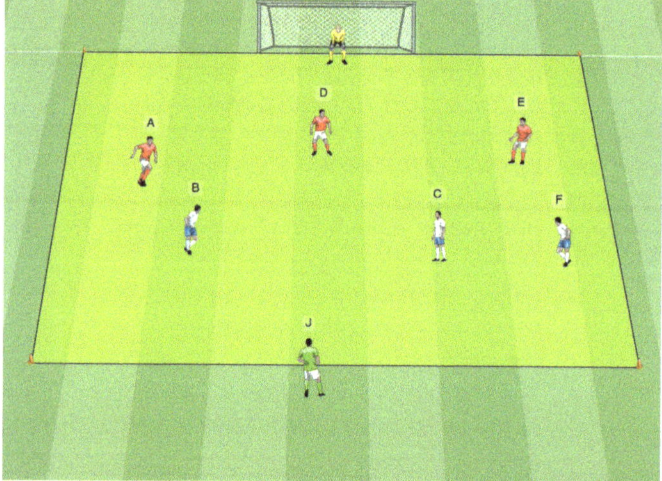

DURATION

24 minutes

OBJECTIVES

- **3 versus 3**
- **Possession**
- **Dismarking**
- **Defensive cover**
- **Finishing**

EQUIPMENT

- **Four cones**
- **Four bibs (three of one color and one of another)**
- **One goal**
- **Balls**

PREPARATION

Playing area: 20-25 x 25x30 meters.
Players: 7 + a goalkeeper.
Number of series: Three of 5 minutes with 3 minutes of recuperation between each series.

ORGANIZATION

In the space chosen for the activity use cones to mark out the playing area. Center a goal on one of the end lines. Divide the players into two teams of three, while the goalkeeper occupies the goal. The neutral player is positioned outside the playing area, across from the goal. The goalkeeper initiates play by passing to one of the two teams, as directed by the coach.

RULES

- Both teams attempt to score on the goal.
- The neutral plays with the team in possession.
- After a goal is scored, the goalkeeper restarts play by throwing the ball to the neutral player on the opposite side of the playing area, who plays to the team that has been scored on.

In the example we see a possible passage of play where a goal scored after a wall pass.

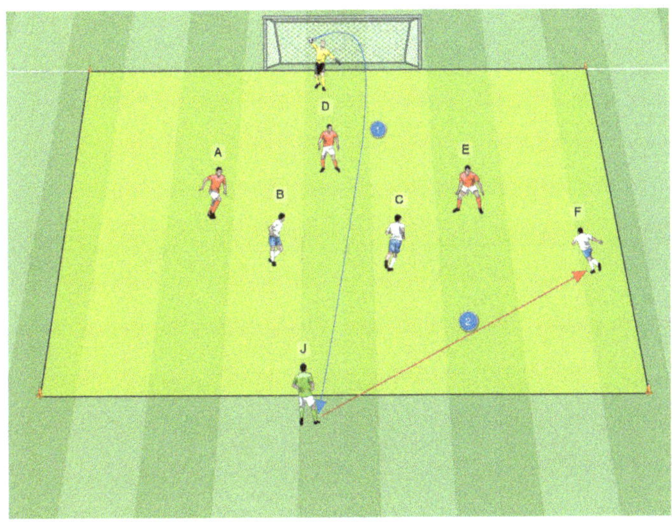

VARIATIONS

1. After a goal is scored, the goalkeeper restarts play by throwing the ball to the neutral player on the opposite side of the playing area, who plays to the team that scored the goal.

2. Limit the players to three touches.

3. The neutral plays with two touches.

<table>
<tr>
<td>COACHING POINTS</td>
<td>

- In possession:
  - Focus on the three versus three situations.
  - This activity imposes a high rhythm of play, training conditional capacities such as specific resistance.
  - Allow the players freedom of action.
  - The players rotate positions after every series.
- Out of possession:
  - Demand high pressure in order to recover the ball as quickly as possible.
  - Balanced defending of the goal, according to collective tactical principles.
  - Players prepared for an attacking transition.
  - The goalkeeper gives verbal instructions to the defenders, and also takes up good positions in goal.

</td>
</tr>
</table>

3 VERSUS 3 + 3 NEUTRALS

04

OPERATING METHOD Small-sided game

DURATION

24 minutes

OBJECTIVES

- Possession
- Width
- Dismarking
- Finishing

EQUIPMENT	PREPARATION
- Four cones - Six bibs (three of one color and three of another) - One goal - Balls	Playing area: 25-30 x 30x35 meters. Players: 9 + a goalkeeper. Number of series: Three of 5 minutes with 3 minutes of recuperation between each series.

ORGANIZATION

In the space chosen for the activity use cones to mark out the playing area. Center a goal on one of the end lines. Divide the players into two teams of three, while the goalkeeper occupies the goal. One neutral player is positioned outside the playing area across from the goal. Two additional neutrals are positioned on the wings; one on each side. The goalkeeper initiates play by passing to one of the neutrals, who plays to one of the two teams, as directed by the coach.

RULES

- Both teams attempt to score on the goal.
- The neutrals play with the team in possession.
- After scoring a goal, the goalkeeper restarts play by throwing the ball to the neutral player on the opposite side of the playing area, who plays to the team that has been scored on.

In the example we can see a possible passage of play which leads to a goal by the white team after a combination with the neutrals.

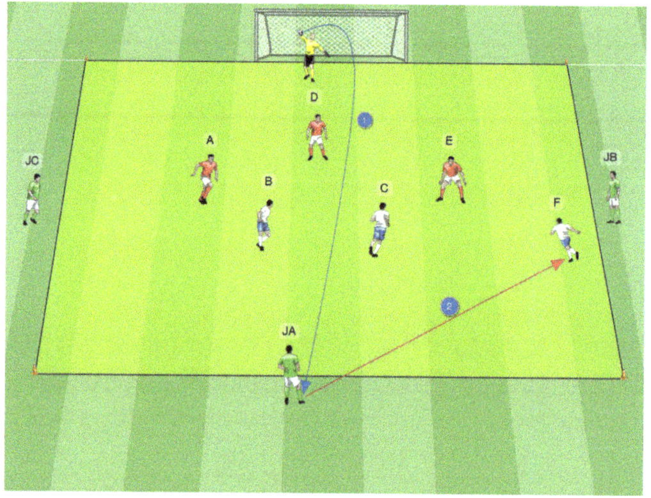

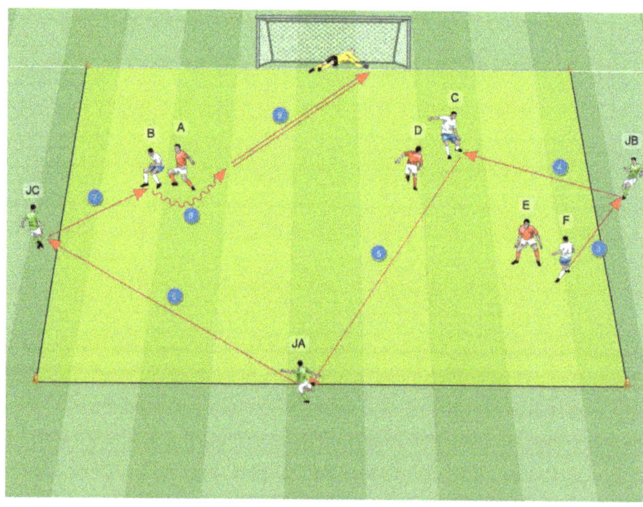

VARIATIONS

1. After a goal is scored, the goalkeeper restarts play by throwing the ball to the neutral player on the opposite side of the playing area, who plays to the team that scored.

2. Limit the players to three touches.

3. The neutral plays with two touches.

<table>
<tr><td>COACHING POINTS</td><td>

- In possession:
  - Focus on the three versus three situations.
  - This activity imposes a high rhythm of play, training conditional capacities such as specific resistance.
  - Allow the players freedom of action.
  - The players rotate positions after every series.
- Out of possession:
  - Demand high pressure in order to recover the ball as quickly as possible.
  - Balanced defending of the goal, according to collective tactical principles.
  - Players prepared for an attacking transition.
  - The goalkeeper gives verbal instructions to the defenders, and also takes up good positions in goal.
</td></tr>
</table>

3 VERSUS 3 WITH 1 NEUTRAL AND 2 EXTERNAL PLAYERS

05

OPERATING METHOD Small-sided game

DURATION

24 minutes

OBJECTIVES

- Possession
- Dismarking
- Width

EQUIPMENT	PREPARATION
- Four cones - Five bibs (four of one color and one of another) - One goal - Balls	Playing area: 25-30 x 30-35 meters. Players: 9 + a goalkeeper. Number of series: Three of 5 minutes with 3 minutes of recuperation between each series.

ORGANIZATION

In the space chosen for the activity use cones to mark out the playing area. Center a goal on one of the end lines. Divide the players into two teams of three, while the goalkeeper occupies the goal. One neutral player is positioned outside the playing area across from the goal. An additional player from each team shall be positioned outside the playing area, on opposite wings. The goalkeeper initiates play by passing to the neutral player, who passes to one of the two teams, as directed by the coach.

RULES

- Both teams attempt to score on the goal.
- The neutral plays with the team in possession.
- When an interior player passes to a exterior teammate, the exterior player carries the ball into the playing area and joins the action; while the player who passed them the ball takes their place on the outside.
- When an interior player passes to the exterior player from the other team, this player simply offers support and remains in their position.
- After scoring a goal, the goalkeeper restarts play by throwing the ball to the neutral player on the opposite side of the playing area, who plays to the team that has been scored on.

In the example you can see a possible passage of play where, after a combination with the supporting player, the white team delivers the ball to the exterior player, who enters the field and overcomes an opponent to score.

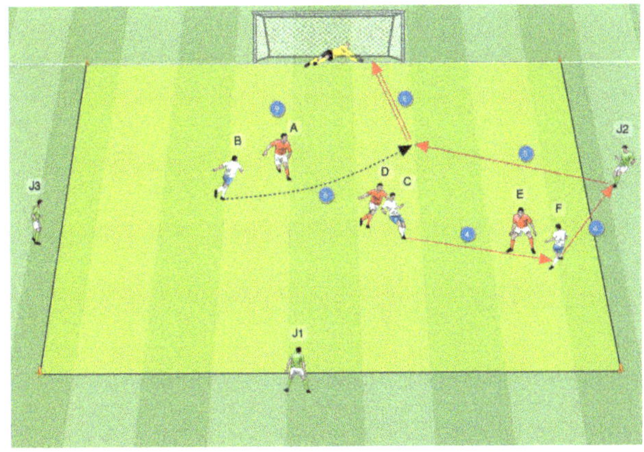

VARIATIONS

1. After a goal is scored, the goalkeeper restarts play by throwing the ball to the neutral player on the opposite side of the playing area, who plays to the team that scored.

2. Limit the players to three touches.

3. The neutral plays with two touches.

4. The external player who enters the playing area may not score.

COACHING POINTS	<ul><li>In possession:<ul><li>Focus on the three versus three situations.</li><li>Allow the players freedom of action.</li><li>The players rotate positions after every series.</li></ul></li><li>Out of possession:<ul><li>Demand high pressure in order to recover the ball as quickly as possible.</li><li>Balanced defending of the goal, according to collective tactical principles.</li><li>Players prepared for an attacking transition.</li><li>The goalkeeper gives verbal instructions to the defenders, and also takes up good positions in goal.</li></ul></li></ul>

FROM 3 VERSUS 2 TO 2 VERSUS 3

06

OPERATING METHOD — Small-sided game

DURATION

22 minutes

OBJECTIVES

- **3 versus 2**
- **Defending the goal**
- **Finishing**
- **Passing**

EQUIPMENT

- **Four cones**
- **Two poles**
- **Five bibs**
- **Two goals**
- **Balls**

PREPARATION

Playing area: 25-30 x 30-40 meters.
Players: 10 + 2 goalkeepers.
Number of series: Two of 8 minutes with 3 minutes of recuperation between series.

ORGANIZATION

In the space chosen for the activity use cones to mark out the playing area. Center a goal on one of the end lines. Use the poles to divide the field into two equal halves, as shown in the illustration. Divide the players into two teams of five, who are arranged in the following manner: two in the defensive zone and three in the attacking zone. The goalkeepers occupy their respective goals. One team initiates possession through their goalkeeper.

RULES

- Play a game with the normal rules of football.

- The players may not change zones; only the ball may move between them.
- The players change positions at the end of each series.

In the example we see a passage of play where the white team scores after starting from their goalkeeper and overcoming the opponent's three attackers and two defenders.

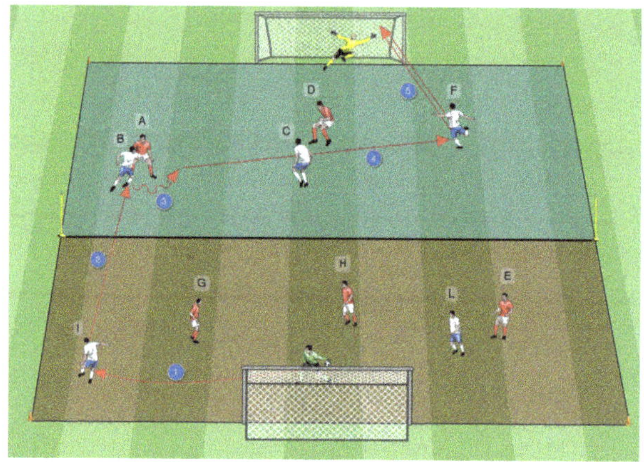

VARIATIONS

1.   One defender can enter the attacking zone.

2.   Limit the players to three touches in the attacking zone.

COACHING POINTS	- In possession:
	  - The players should occupy different depths to allow them to maintain balance and play quickly in both phases of the game.
	  - Demand a high rhythm of play from the players to improve their aerobic capacity.
	  - Encourage vertical play.
	  - Allow the players the freedom to take opponents on 1 versus 1.
	- Out of possession:
	  - Demand high pressure in order to recover the ball as quickly as possible.
	  - Balanced defending of the goal, according to collective tactical principles.
	  - Players prepared for an attacking transition.
	  - The goalkeeper gives verbal instructions to the defenders, and also takes up good positions in goal.

FROM 2 VERSUS 3 TO 3 VERSUS 2 WITH 2 NEUTRALS

07

OPERATING METHOD Small-sided game

DURATION

22 minutes

OBJECTIVES

- **3 versus 2**
- **Defending the goal**
- **Possession**
- **Width**
- **Finishing**

EQUIPMENT

- **Four cones and two poles**
- **Seven bibs (five of one color and two of another)**
- **Two goals**
- **Balls**

PREPARATION

Playing area: 25-30 x 30-40 meters.
Players: 12 + 2 goalkeepers.
Number of series: Two of 8 minutes with 3 minutes of recuperation between series.

ORGANIZATION

In the space chosen for the activity use cones to mark out the playing area. Center a goal on one of the end lines. Use the poles to divide the field into two equal halves, as shown in the illustration. Divide the players into two teams of five, who are arranged in the following manner: two in the defensive zone and three in the attacking zone. The goalkeepers occupy their respective goals. The neutrals are positioned on the wings, one on each side. One team initiates possession through their goalkeeper

.RULES

- Play a game with the normal rules of football.
- The players may not change zones; only the ball may move between them.
- The neutrals play with the team in possession.
- The player change positions at the end of each series.

In the example we see a passage of play where the white team scores after starting from their goalkeeper and overcoming the opponent's three attackers and two defenders.

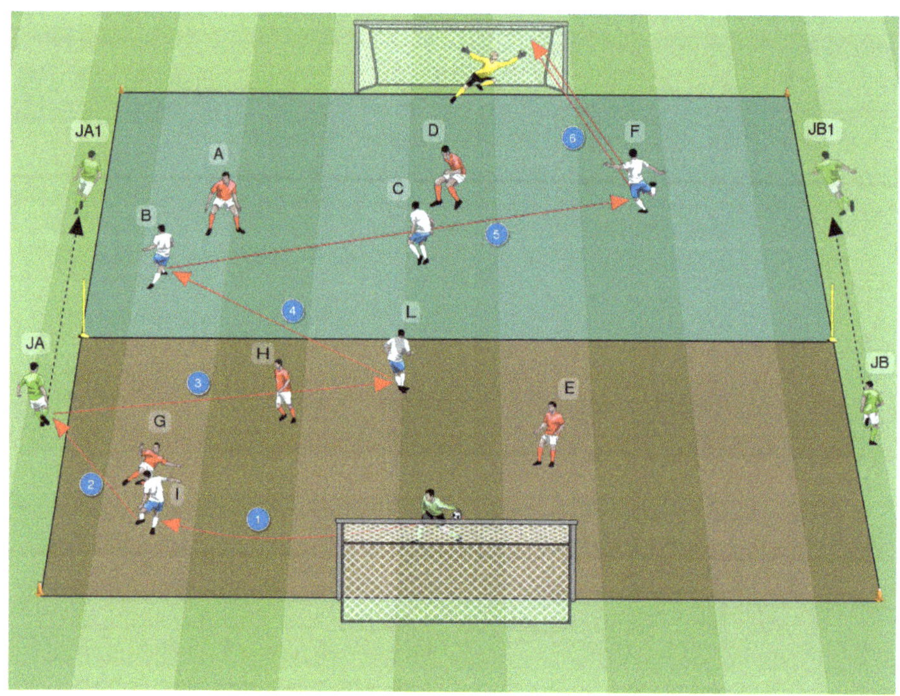

VARIATIONS

1. One defender can enter the attacking zone.

2. Limit the players to three touches in the attacking zone.

<table>
<tr><td>COACHING POINTS</td><td>

- In possession:
  - The players should occupy different depths to allow them to maintain balance and play quickly in both phases of the game.
  - Encourage the use of the neutrals to create situations of numerical superiority.
  - Encourage vertical play.
  - Allow the players the freedom to take opponents on 1 versus 1.
- Out of possession:
  - Demand high pressure in order to recover the ball as quickly as possible.
  - Balanced defending of the goal, according to collective tactical principles.
  - Players prepared for an attacking transition.
  - The goalkeeper gives verbal instructions to the defenders, and also takes up good positions in goal.

</td></tr>
</table>

3 VERSUS 2 ON TWO FIELDS

08

OPERATING METHOD Small-sided game

DURATION

24 minutes

OBJECTIVES

- 3 versus 2
- Finishing
- Defensive cover
- Possession

EQUIPMENT	PREPARATION
- Eight cones - Four bibs - Two goals - Balls	Playing area: 25-30 x 30-40 meters. Players: 10 + 2 goalkeepers. Number of series: Three of 5 minutes with 3 minutes of recuperationbetween each series.

ORGANIZATION

Set up two 20x25 meter playing areas. Position two goals back-to-back on the end lines between the two rectangles (as shown in the illustration). Divide the players into two teams; one team of six players and another of four players. Organize three forwards and two defenders on each field, in a way that creates a pair of three versus two situations. The goalkeepers occupy their respective goals. A goalkeeper initiates play by passing to the team in numerical superiority.

RULES

- Play using the normal rules of football. The attackers can score in both goals.
- The players may not change zones; only the ball may move between them.
- The players may pass the ball to their teammates on the other side.
- After a goal is scored, the goalkeeper passes to the team in numerical superiority to restart play.
- If the defenders recover the ball and play to the goalkeeper, they earn a point.
- Players change positions after every series.

In the example we see a possible passage of play where the team in white finishes after receiving the ball from the goalkeeper and passing to the other zone.

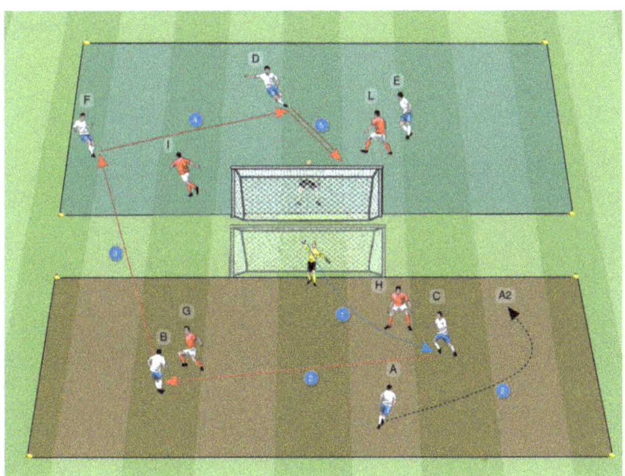

VARIATIONS

1. One defender can change zones when the ball is not in their area to create a three versus three.

2. Limit the players on the attacking team to three touches.

COACHING POINTS	<ul><li>Train the reaction to the defensive transition: the player closest to where the ball is lost should press the opponent while the teammates reduce the space.</li><li>The player closest to the ball carrier must decide what to do: move towards the ball or away from it.</li><li>Avoid having the players position themselves on the same line, in order to ensure balance when combining.</li></ul>

3 VERSUS 2 SUPERIORITY WITH A TEAMMATE IN SUPPORT

09

OPERATING METHOD Small-sided game

DURATION

24 minutes

OBJECTIVES

- 3 versus 3
- Finishing
- Switching play
- Defensive cover

EQUIPMENT	PREPARATION
<ul><li>Eight cones</li><li>Five bibs</li><li>Two goals</li><li>Balls</li></ul>	Playing area: 25-30 x 30-40 meters. Players: 10 + 2 goalkeepers. Number of series: Three of 5 minutes with 3 minutes of recuperation between each series.

ORGANIZATION

Set up two 20x25 meter playing areas. Position two goals back-to-back on the end lines between the two rectangles (as shown in the illustration). Divide the players into two teams of five; each with three forwards in one zone and two defenders in the other (to create a pair of three versus two situations). The goalkeepers occupy their respective goals. Play starts in the zone determined by the coach, with the goalkeeper passing to the team in numerical superiority.

RULES

- Play using normal the normal rules of football. The teams can score in both goals.
- The attackers look to score in both zones.
- When the defenders recover the ball, they must pass it to a teammate in the other zone.
- One attacker at a time can change zones, when the ball is not in their area, to help the defenders by creating a three versus three situation. If the ball is recovered by the opponent and switched to the other side, this player must return to their zone.
- After a goal, the goalkeeper passes to the team in numerical superiority to restart play.

In the example we see a possible passage of play, with the white team finishing after recovering the ball and delivering it to the other side.

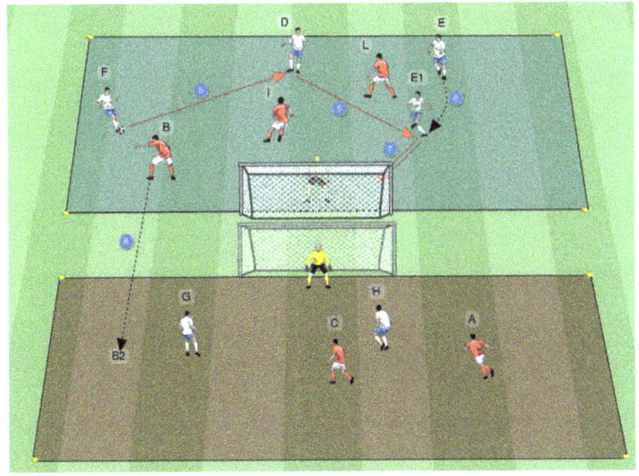

VARIATIONS

1. The attackers are limited to three touches.

COACHING POINTS	<ul><li>Train the reaction to the defensive transition: the player closest to where the ball is lost should press the opponent while the teammates reduce the space.</li><li>Train the collective spacing of the players.</li><li>The player closest to the ball carrier must decide what to do: move towards the ball or away from it, according to the actions of their teammate.</li><li>Avoid having the players position themselves on the same line, in order to ensure balance when combining.</li></ul>

3 VERSUS 2 ON TWO FIELDS WITH 2 EXTERNAL NEUTRALS

10

OPERATING METHOD Small-sided game

DURATION

24 minutes

OBJECTIVES

- 3 versus 2
- Finishing
- Defending the goal
- Dismarking
- 3 versus 2

EQUIPMENT	PREPARATION
<ul><li>Eight cones</li><li>Seven bibs (five of one color and two of another)</li><li>Two goals</li><li>Balls</li></ul>	Playing area: 25-30 x 30-40 meters. Players: 12 + 2 goalkeepers. Number of series: Three of 5 minutes with 3 minutes of recuperation between each series.

ORGANIZATION

Set up two 30x25 meter playing areas. Position two goals back-to-back on the end lines between the two rectangles (as shown in the illustration). Divide the players into two teams of five, each with three forwards in one zone and two defenders in the other (to create a pair of three versus two situations). Each team attacks in one zone and defends in the other. The goalkeepers occupy their respective goals. Two neutral players are positioned on the wings, outside the playing areas. Play starts in the zone determined by the coach, with the goalkeeper passing to the team in numerical superiority.

RULES

- Play using the normal rules of football. The teams can score in both goals.
- The neutrals play with the team in possession.
- The attackers look to score in both zones.
- When the defenders recover the ball, they may pass it to a teammate in the other zone.
- One attacker at a time can change zones, when the ball is not in their area, to help the defenders by creating a three versus three situation. If the ball is recovered by the opponent and switched to the other side, this player must return to their zone.
- After a goal is scored, the goalkeeper passes to the team in numerical superiority to restart play.

In the example we see a possible passage of play, with a finish by the white team after recovering possession and delivering the ball to the other side.

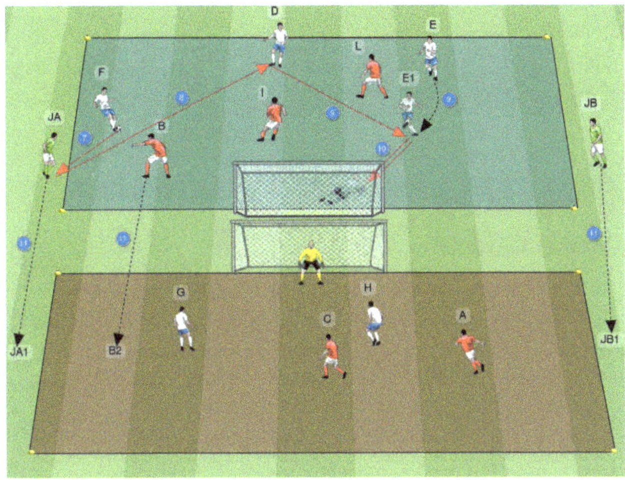

VARIATIONS

1. The attackers are limited to three touches.

COACHING POINTS

- Train the reaction to the defensive transition: the player closest to where the ball is lost should press the opponent while the teammates reduce the space.
- Train the collective spacing of the players.
- The player closest to the ball carrier must decide what to do: move towards the ball or away from it, according to the actions of their teammate.
- Avoid having the players position themselves on the same line, in order to ensure balance when combining.

3 VERSUS 2 ON TWO FIELDS WITH TWO EXTERIOR TEAMMATES

11

OPERATING METHOD Small-sided game

DURATION

24 minutes

OBJECTIVES

- 3 versus 3
- Defending the goal
- Finishing
- Switching play

EQUIPMENT	PREPARATION
<ul><li>Eight cones</li><li>Six bibs</li><li>Two goals</li><li>Balls</li></ul>	Playing area: 25-30 x 30-40 meters. Players: 12 + 2 goalkeepers. Number of series: Three of 5 minutes with 3 minutes of recuperation between each series.

ORGANIZATION

Set up two 25x15 meter playing areas. Position two goals back-to-back on the end lines between the two rectangles (as shown in the illustration). Divide the players into two teams of six, with three forwards in one zone and two defenders in the other (to create a pair of three versus two situations). Each team attacks in one zone and defends in the other. The goalkeepers occupy their respective goals. Each team also has an extra player positioned outside the playing areas, on opposite wings. Play starts in the zone determined by the coach, with the goalkeeper passing to the team in numerical superiority.

RULES

- Play using the normal rules of football.
- The attackers look to score in both zones.
- When the defenders recover the ball, they may pass it to a teammate in the other zone.
- One attacker at a time can change zones, when the ball is not in their area, to help the defenders by creating a three versus three situation. If the ball is recovered by the opponent and switched to the other side, this player must return to their zone.
- When an interior player passes to an exterior player of the same color, the receiver carries the ball into the playing area, while the passer replaces them on the outside.
- When an interior player passes to an exterior player of a different color, the receiver only plays a supporting role and remains in their position.
- The external players may move along the entire length of the sideline.
- After a goal is scored, the goalkeeper passes to the team in numerical superiority to restart play.
- The players change positions after every series.

In the example we see a possible passage of play, with a finish by the white team after receiving the ball from the goalkeeper and passing to the opposite side.

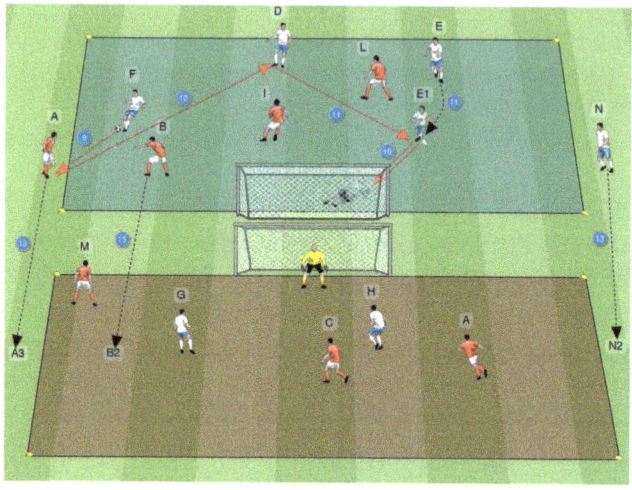

VARIATIONS

1. The attackers are limited to three touches.

COACHING POINTS	• Avoid having the players position themselves on the same line, in order to ensure balance when combining. • The switching of zones required in this activity train components of conditioning, such as specific resistance.

3 VERSUS 3 + 2 EXTERIOR ATTACKING TEAMMATES

12

DURATION

14 minutes

OBJECTIVES

- **Transitions**
- **Defending the goal**
- **Finishing**

EQUIPMENT	PREPARATION
<ul><li>Cones to mark out the playing area</li><li>Four bibs</li><li>Two goals</li><li>Balls</li></ul>	Playing area: 25-30 x 30-40 meters. Players: 9 + 2 goalkeepers. Number of series: Two of 5 minutes with 2 minutes of recuperation between each series.

ORGANIZATION

In the space chosen for the activity set up a playing area and divide it in half. Position a goal on each end line. Divide the players into two teams; one team of four defenders (in red bibs), who are arranged in pairs in each half, and another team of five attackers (in white bibs) who all occupy one half of the field. Two of the attackers are initially positioned in the channels outside of the playing area, one on each side. The two goalkeepers occupy their respective goals. Play starts with one of the two goalkeepers serving the ball by hand to one of the attackers.

RULES

- The defenders may only leave their half of the field (one at a time) to help defend when the action is developing on the other side.
- After the sequence is finished or the ball is recovered, this player must quickly return to their zone.
- The attackers can score in either goal, except after receiving the ball from the goalkeeper at the start of play. In that situation, they must score in the opposite goal.
- When an exterior player receives the ball, they dribble the ball into the playing area, while the player making the pass takes their place on the outside.
- If the defenders recover the ball, they must evade their opponents and dribble the ball out of the playing area.
- The players change positions after every series.

In the example we see a possible passage of play, with the white attackers scoring after playing to an exterior player.

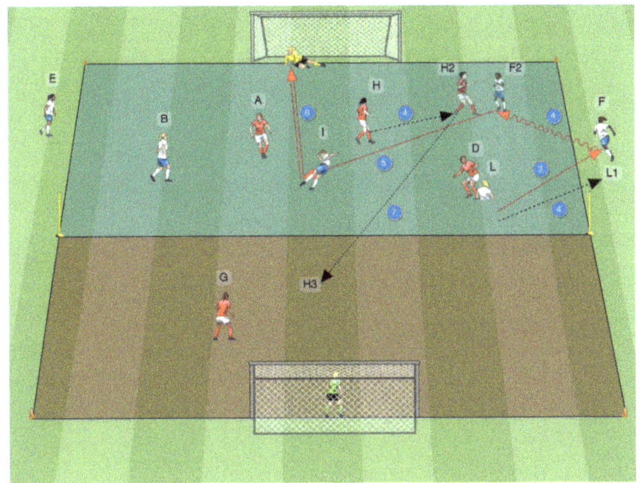

VARIATIONS

1. Touch limitations.

2. The goalkeepers can play with the defenders.

<table>
<tr><td>COACHING POINTS</td><td>

- The attacking players must be encouraged to finish with a shot on goal as quickly as possible.
- The initial numerical superiority facilitates rapid finishing.
- Train the collective spacing of the players.
- Always provide the player in possession with at least two options, especially options in support and to lay the ball off.
- If the player in possession is in a "free ball" situation, the players without the ball should attack space in a pre-set manner.
- After the player in possession releases the ball, they must move and make themselves available again.

</td></tr>
</table>

FROM 3 VERSUS 2 TO 3 VERSUS 4: SCORE IN BOTH GOALS

13

OPERATING METHOD Small-sided game

DURATION

24 minutes

OBJECTIVES

- Transitions
- Finishing
- Possession

EQUIPMENT	PREPARATION
<ul><li>Four cones</li><li>Two poles</li><li>Four bibs</li><li>Two goals</li><li>Balls</li></ul>	Playing area: 25-30 x 30-40 meters. Players: 7 + 2 goalkeepers. Number of series: Three of 5 minutes with 3 minutes of recuperation between each series.

ORGANIZATION

In the space chosen for the activity use cones to set up the playing area. Place a goal on each end line. Divide the field into two equal halves, marking the midway point with poles. Divide the players into two teams; one team of four (with two players positioned in each half) and one team of three. The goalkeepers occupy their respective goals. One of the goalkeepers initiates play.

RULES

- The goalkeeper starts play with ball in hand, serving it to the team of three players who face their opponents in the opposite half of the field.

- The defenders may not leave their zones.
- The team in numerical inferiority can score in either of the two goals.
- When the defenders recover the ball, they must try to maintain possession.
- After scoring a goal, the team of three players receives the ball from the goalkeeper on the opposite side and attacks again.

In the example we see a possible passage of play that ends with a goal for the white team.

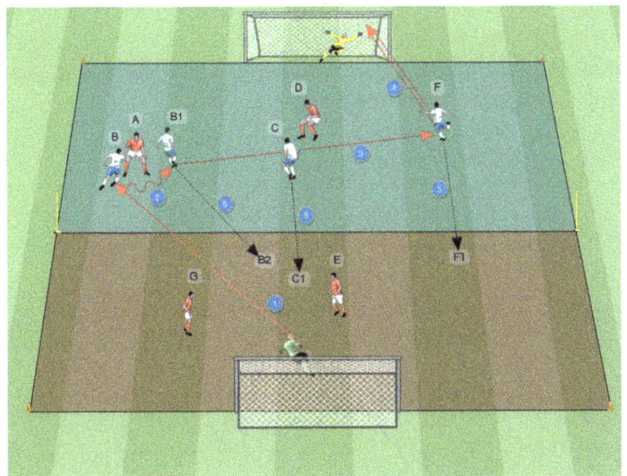

VARIATIONS

1. The players must keep the ball on the ground.

COACHING POINTS	<ul><li>Train the reaction to the defensive transition: the player closest to where the ball is lost should press the opponent while the teammates reduce the space.</li><li>Train the collective spacing of the players.</li><li>Avoid having the players position themselves on the same line, in order to ensure balance when combining.</li><li>Always provide the player in possession with at least two passing options.</li><li>If the player in possession is in a "free ball" situation, the players without the ball should attack space in a pre-set manner.</li><li>After the player in possession releases the ball, they must move and make themselves available again.</li></ul>

FROM 3 VERSUS 2 TO 3 VERSUS 4 WITH 2 NEUTRALS: SCORE IN BOTH GOALS

14

OPERATING METHOD | **Small-sided game**

DURATION

22 minutes

OBJECTIVES

- **Transitions**
- **Finishing**
- **Possession**
- **3 versus 2**

EQUIPMENT	PREPARATION
<ul><li>Four cones and two poles</li><li>Six bibs (four of one color and two of another)</li><li>Two goals</li><li>Balls</li></ul>	Playing area: 25-30 x 30-40 meters. Players: 9 + 2 goalkeepers. Number of series: Three of 5 minutes with 3 minutes of recuperation between each series.

ORGANIZATION

In the space chosen for the activity use cones to set up the playing area. Place a goal on each end line. Divide the field into two equal halves, marking the midway point with poles. Divide the players into two teams; one team of four (with two players positioned in each half) and one team of three. The goalkeepers occupy their respective goals. Two neutrals in bibs of another color are positioned in the wide areas, one on each side. One of the goalkeepers initiates play.

RULES

- The goalkeeper starts play with ball in hand, serving it to the team of three players who face their opponents in the opposite half of the field.

- The defenders may not leave their zones.
- The team in numerical inferiority can score in either of the two goals.
- The neutrals play with the team in possession and are limited to three touches.
- The neutrals may not run with the ball.
- The neutrals may not score.
- When the defenders recover the ball, they must try to maintain possession.
- After scoring a goal, the team of three players receives the ball from the goalkeeper on the opposite side and attacks again.

In the example we see a possible passage of play that ends with a goal for the white team.

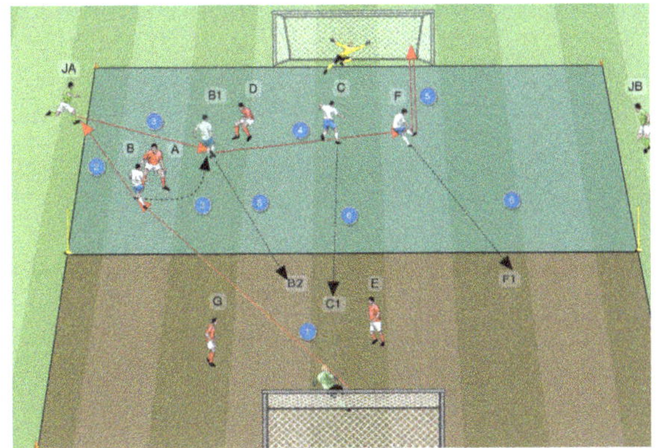

VARIATIONS

1. The players must keep the ball on the ground.

2. The neutrals are limited to three touches.

COACHING POINTS	- Train the reaction to the defensive transition: the player closest to where the ball is lost should press the opponent while the teammates reduce the space. - Always provide the player in possession with at least two passing options. - If the player in possession is in a "free ball" situation, the players without the ball should attack space in a pre-set manner. - After the player in possession releases the ball, they must move and make themselves available again.

FROM 3 VERSUS 2 TO 3 VERSUS 4 WITH 2 EXTERIOR TEAMMATES: SCORE IN BOTH GOALS

15

OPERATING METHOD Small-sided game

DURATION

24 minutes

OBJECTIVES

- Transitions
- 3 versus 2
- Finishing
- Possession

EQUIPMENT	PREPARATION
<ul><li>Four cones and two poles</li><li>Seven bibs (five of one color and two of another)</li><li>Two goals</li><li>Balls</li></ul>	Playing area: 25-30 x 30-40 meters. Players: 9 + 2 goalkeepers. Number of series: Two of 8 minutes with 3 minutes of recuperation between series.

ORGANIZATION

In the space chosen for the activity use cones to set up the playing area. Place a goal on each end line. Divide the field into two equal halves, marking the midway point with poles. Divide the players into two teams; one team of five (with three interior players and two supporting players positioned on the wings) and one team of four (with two players positioned in each half). The goalkeepers occupy their respective goals. One of the goalkeepers initiates play.

RULES

- The goalkeeper starts play with ball in hand, serving it to the team of three players who face their opponents in the opposite half of the field.
- The defenders may not leave their zones.
- The team in numerical inferiority can score in either of the two goals.
- When the defenders recover the ball, they must try to maintain possession.
- When an exterior teammate receives the ball, they dribble it into the playing area, while the interior teammate who made the pass takes their place on the outside.
- When the defenders recover the ball, the exterior players support them to create a six versus three.
- The exterior players may not run with the ball.
- After scoring a goal, the team of three players receives the ball from the goalkeeper on the opposite side and attacks again.

In the example we see a possible passage of play that ends with a goal for the white team.

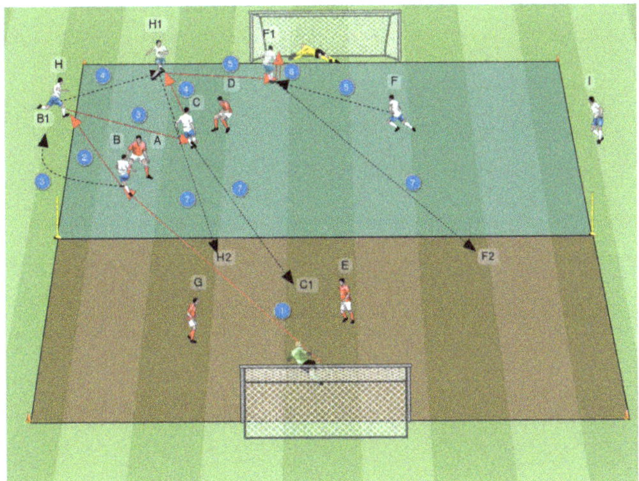

VARIATIONS

1. The players must keep the ball on the ground.
2. The exterior players are limited to two touches.

COACHING POINTS	<ul><li>Train the reaction to the defensive transition: the player closest to where the ball is lost should press the opponent while the teammates reduce the space.</li><li>Always provide the player in possession with at least two passing options.</li><li>If the player in possession is in a "free ball" situation, the players without the ball should attack space in a pre-set manner.</li><li>After the player in possession releases the ball, they must move and make themselves available again.</li></ul>

FROM 3 VERSUS 3 TO 3 VERSUS 4: SCORE IN BOTH GOALS

16

OPERATING METHOD Small-sided game

DURATION

24 minutes

OBJECTIVES

- Transitions
- 3 versus 3
- Finishing
- Possession

EQUIPMENT	PREPARATION
- Four cones - Two poles - Four bibs - Two goals - Balls	Playing area: 25-30 x 30-40 meters. Players: 7 + 2 goalkeepers. Number of series: Three of 5 minutes with 3 minutes of recuperation between each series.

ORGANIZATION

In the space chosen for the activity use cones to set up the playing area. Place a goal on each end line. Divide the field into two equal halves, marking the midway point with poles. Divide the players into two teams; one team of four (with two players positioned in each half) and one team of three. The goalkeepers occupy their respective goals. One of the goalkeepers initiates play.

RULES

- The goalkeeper starts play with ball in hand, serving it to the team of three players who face their opponents in the opposite half of the field.
- One of the defending players can go to help their teammates on the opposite side when the action is developing there, but they must return to their zone after the ball is recovered or a goal is scored.
- The team in numerical inferiority can score in either of the two goals.
- When the defenders recover the ball, they must try to maintain possession.
- After scoring a goal, the team of three players receives the ball from the goalkeeper on the opposite side and attacks again.

In the example we see a possible passage of play that ends with a goal for the white team.

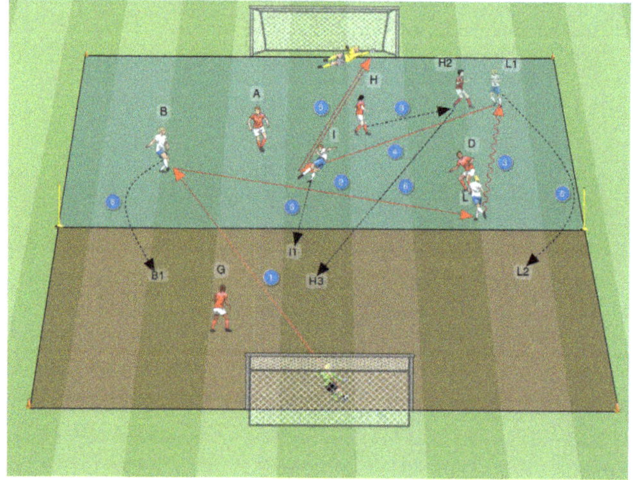

VARIATIONS

1. The players must keep the ball on the ground.

COACHING POINTS

- Train the reaction to the defensive transition: the player closest to where the ball is lost should press the opponent while the teammates reduce the space.
- Train the collective spacing of the players.
- Avoid having the players position themselves on the same line, in order to ensure balance when combining.
- If the player in possession is in a "free ball" situation, the players without the ball should attack space in a pre-set manner.
- After the player in possession releases the ball, they must move and make themselves available again.

FROM 3 VERSUS 2 TO 3 VERSUS 4 WITH 2 EXTERNAL NEUTRALS: SCORE IN BOTH GOALS

17

OPERATING METHOD Small-sided game

DURATION

24 minutes

OBJECTIVES

- Transitions
- 3 versus 3
- Possession
- Finishing

EQUIPMENT

- Four cones and two poles
- Six bibs (four of one color and two of another)
- Two goals
- One ball

PREPARATION

Playing area: 25-30 x 30-40 meters.
Players: 9 + 2 goalkeepers.
Number of series: Three of 5 minutes with 3 minutes of recuperation between each series.

ORGANIZATION

In the space chosen for the activity use cones to set up the playing area. Place a goal on each end line. Divide the field into two equal halves, marking the midway point with poles. Divide the players into two teams; one team of four (with two players positioned in each half) and one team of three. Two neutrals in bibs of another color are positioned in the wide areas, one on each side. The goalkeepers occupy their respective goals. One of the goalkeepers initiates play.

RULES

- The goalkeeper starts play with ball in hand, serving it to the team of three players who face their opponents in the opposite half of the field.
- The neutrals play with the team in possession.
- One of the defending players can go to help their teammates on the opposite side when the action is developing there, but they must return to their zone after the ball is recovered or a goal is scored.
- The team in numerical inferiority can score in either of the two goals.
- When the defenders recover the ball, they must try to maintain possession.
- After scoring a goal, the team of three players receives the ball from the goalkeeper on the opposite side and attacks again.
- The neutrals may not run with the ball.

In the example we see a possible passage of play in which the white team scores after combining with an exterior neutral.

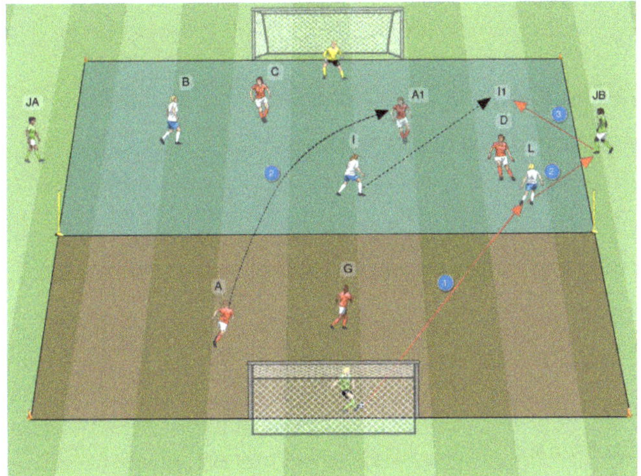

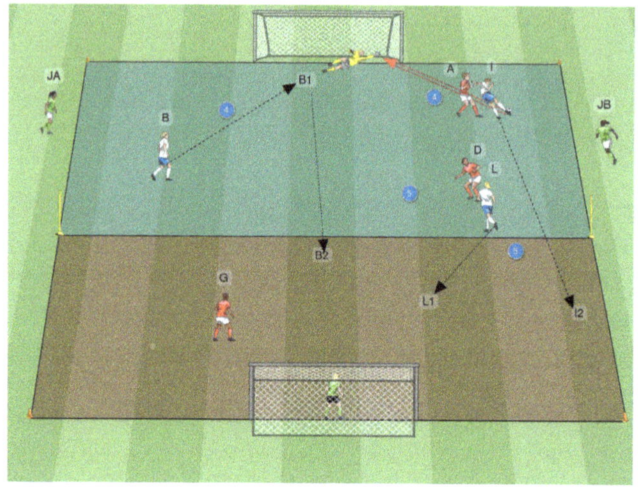

VARIATIONS

1. The players must keep the ball on the ground.

2. The neutrals are limited to two touches.

COACHING POINTS	<ul><li>Avoid having the players position themselves on the same line, in order to ensure balance when combining.</li><li>If the player in possession is in a "free ball" situation, the players without the ball should attack space in a pre-set manner.</li><li>After the player in possession releases the ball, they must move and make themselves available again.</li></ul>

FROM 3 VERSUS 3 TO 3 VERSUS 4 WITH 2 TEAMMATES: SCORE IN BOTH GOALS

18

OPERATING METHOD   Small-sided game

DURATION

24 minutes

OBJECTIVES

- **Transitions**
- **Possession**
- **3 versus 3**
- **Finishing**

EQUIPMENT	PREPARATION
- **Four cones** - **Two poles** - **Four bibs** - **Two goals** - **Balls**	**Playing area: 25-30 x 30-40 meters.** **Players: 9 + 2 goalkeepers.** **Number of series: Three of 5 minutes** **with 3 minutes of recuperation** **between each series.**

ORGANIZATION

In the space chosen for the activity use cones to set up the playing area. Place a goal on each end line. Divide the field into two equal halves, marking the midway point with poles. Divide the players into two teams; one team of four (with two players positioned in each half) and one team of five (with three players inside the playing area and two one the outside; one on each wing). The goalkeepers occupy their respective goals. One of the goalkeepers initiates play.

RULES

- The goalkeeper starts play with ball in hand, serving it to the team of three players who face their opponents in the opposite half of the field.
- The exterior players play with the team in possession.
- When an exterior teammate receives the ball, they dribble it into the playing area, while the interior teammate who made the pass takes their place on the outside.
- When an interior player passes to an exterior player of a different color, the receiver only plays a supporting role and remains in their position.
- One of the defending players can go to help their teammates on the opposite side when the action is developing there, but they must return to their zone after the ball is recovered or a goal is scored.
- The team in numerical inferiority can score in either of the two goals.
- When the defenders recover the ball, they must try to maintain possession.
- After scoring a goal, the team of three players receives the ball from the goalkeeper on the opposite side and attacks again.
- The neutrals may not run with the ball.

In the example we see a possible passage of play in which the white team scores after an interchange between the exterior player (H), who enters the playing area, and player (L) who takes their place after passing them the ball.

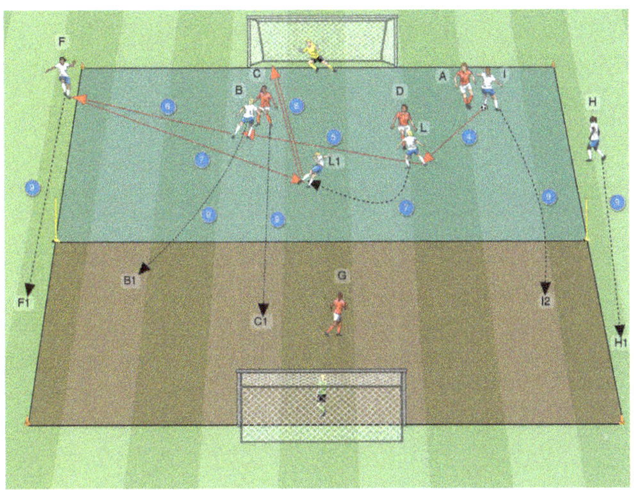

VARIATIONS

1. The players must keep the ball on the ground.

2. The exterior players are limited to two touches.

COACHING POINTS	<ul><li>Avoid having the players position themselves on the same line, in order to ensure balance when combining.</li><li>If the player in possession is in a "free ball" situation, the players without the ball should attack space in a pre-set manner.</li><li>After the player in possession releases the ball, they must move and make themselves available again.</li></ul>

3 VERSUS 4: LOOKING TO FINISH QUICKLY

19

OPERATING METHOD Small-sided game

DURATION

14 minutes

OBJECTIVES

- **Finishing**
- **Possession**
- **Transitions**

EQUIPMENT	PREPARATION
- **Cones to mark out the playing area** - **Four bibs** - **Two goals** - **Balls**	**Playing area: 25-30 x 30-40 meters.** **Players: 7 + 2 goalkeepers.** **Number of series: Two of 5 minutes with 2 minutes of recuperation between series.**

ORGANIZATION

In the space chosen for the activity use cones to set up the playing area. Place a goal on each end line. Divide the field into two equal halves, marking the midway point with poles. Divide the players into two teams; one team of four defenders (in red bibs, with two players positioned in each half) and one team of three attackers (in white shirts, who all start in the same zone). The goalkeepers occupy their respective goals. One of the goalkeepers initiates play by passing to an attacker, who attacks the opposite goal.

RULES

- The defenders may only leave their half of the field (one at a time) to help defend when the action is developing on the other side.
- After the sequence is finished or the ball is recovered, this player must quickly return to their zone.
- The attackers can score in either goal, except after receiving the ball from the goalkeeper at the start of play. In that situation, they must score in the opposite goal.
- The attackers can repeatedly change the goal they want to attack, looking for the best opportunities to score.
- When the defenders recover the ball, they must try to maintain possession.
- Players change positions after every series.

In the example we see a possible passage of play in which the attacking team scores.

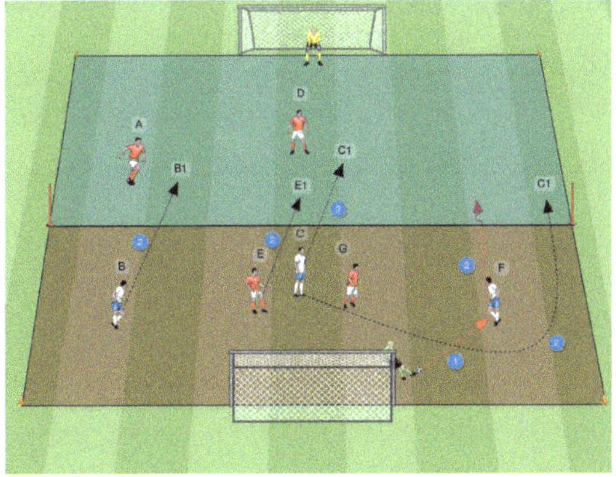

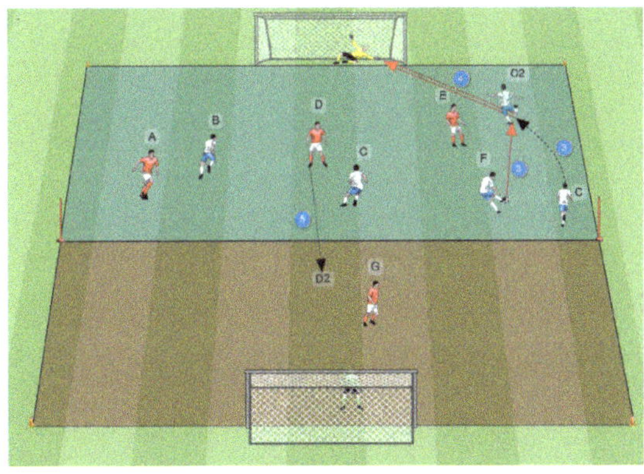

VARIATIONS

1. The goalkeepers can help the defending team keep possession.

COACHING POINTS	<ul><li>Encourage the players to finish with a shot on goal as quickly as possible.</li><li>The initial numerical superiority facilitates rapid finishing.</li><li>In situations of momentary numerical inferiority, the defenders must mark the player with the ball and cover their teammate.</li><li>Avoid having the players position themselves on the same line, in order to guarantee balance when combining.</li><li>Always provide the player in possession with at least two passing options.</li><li>After the player in possession releases the ball, they must move and make themselves available again.</li></ul>

3 VERSUS 4 WITH AN INTERIOR NEUTRAL

20

OPERATING METHOD Small-sided game

DURATION

12 minutes

OBJECTIVES

- **Transitions**
- **Possession**
- **Finishing**

EQUIPMENT

- **Cones to mark out the playing area**
- **Five bibs (four of one color and one of another)**
- **Two goals**
- **Balls**

PREPARATION

Playing area: 25-30 x 30-40 meters.
Players: 8 + 2 goalkeepers.
Number of series: Two of 5 minutes with 2 minutes of recuperation between series.

ORGANIZATION

In the space chosen for the activity use cones to set up the playing area. Place a goal on each end line. Divide the field into two equal halves, marking the midway point with poles. Divide the players into two teams; one team of four defenders (in red bibs, with two players positioned in each half) and one team of three attackers (in white shirts, who all start in the same zone). A neutral player (in green bib) starts in the same zone as the attackers. The goalkeepers occupy their respective goals. One of the goalkeepers initiates play by passing to an attacker, who attacks the opposite goal.

RULES

- The defenders may only leave their half of the field (one at a time) to help defend when the action is developing on the other side.
- After the sequence is finished or the ball is recovered, this player must quickly return to their zone.
- The attackers can score in either goal, except after receiving the ball from the goalkeeper at the start of play. In that situation, they must score in the opposite goal.
- The neutral player plays with the team in possession.
- When the defenders recover the ball, they must try to maintain possession.
- Players change positions after every series.

In the example we see a possible passage of play in which the white team scores with the help of the neutral player.

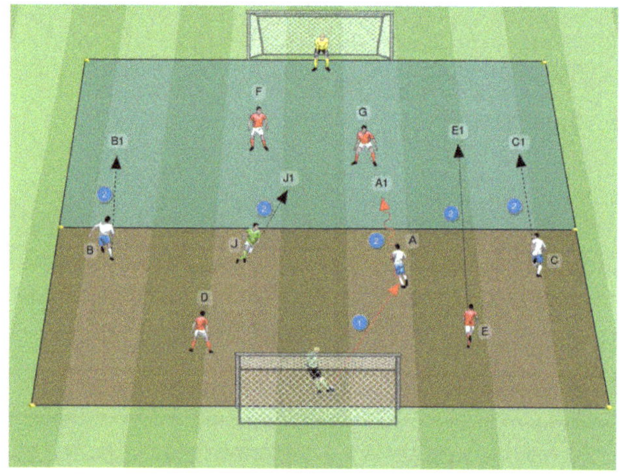

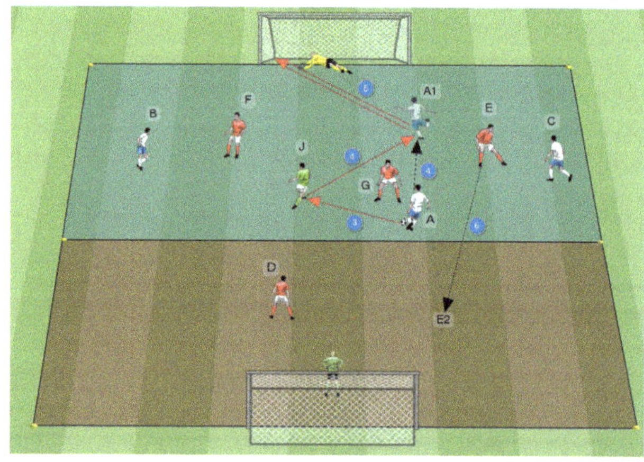

VARIATIONS

1. Touch limits.

2. Touch limits for the neutral.

3. The goalkeepers can play with the defenders to keep possession.

COACHING POINTS	<ul><li>Encourage the players to finish with a shot on goal as quickly as possible.</li><li>The initial numerical superiority facilitates rapid finishing.</li><li>Encourage the defenders to take up good positions to compensate for their numerical inferiority.</li><li>Train the collective spacing of the players.</li><li>If the player in possession is in a "free ball" situation, the players without the ball should attack space in a pre-set manner.</li><li>After the player in possession releases the ball, they must move and make themselves available again.</li></ul>

3 VERSUS 4 WITH 2 EXTERIOR NEUTRALS

21

OPERATING METHOD Small-sided game

DURATION

14 minutes

OBJECTIVES

- Finishing
- Possession
- Passing

EQUIPMENT	PREPARATION
- Cones to mark out the playing area - Six bibs (four of one color and two of another) - Two goals - Balls	Playing area: 25-30 x 30-40 meters. Players: 9 + 2 goalkeepers. Number of series: Two of 5 minutes with 2 minutes of recuperation between series.

ORGANIZATION

In the space chosen for the activity use cones to set up the playing area. Place a goal on each end line. Divide the field into two equal halves, marking the midway point with poles. Divide the players into two teams; one team of four defenders (in red bibs, with two players positioned in each half) and one team of three attackers (in white shirts, who all start in the same zone). The two neutral players (in green bibs) are positioned outside the playing area, on opposite wings. The goalkeepers occupy their respective goals. One of the goalkeepers initiates play by passing to an attacker, who attacks the opposite goal.

RULES

- The defenders may only leave their half of the field (one at a time) to help defend when the action is developing on the other side.
- After the sequence is finished or the ball is recovered, this player must quickly return to their zone.
- When the defenders recover the ball, they must try to maintain possession.
- The attackers can score in either goal, except after receiving the ball from the goalkeeper at the start of play. In that situation, they must score in the opposite goal.
- The neutrals play with the team in possession.
- Players change positions after every series.

In the example we see a possible passage of play, with a shot on goal by the white team after a pass from one of the neutrals.

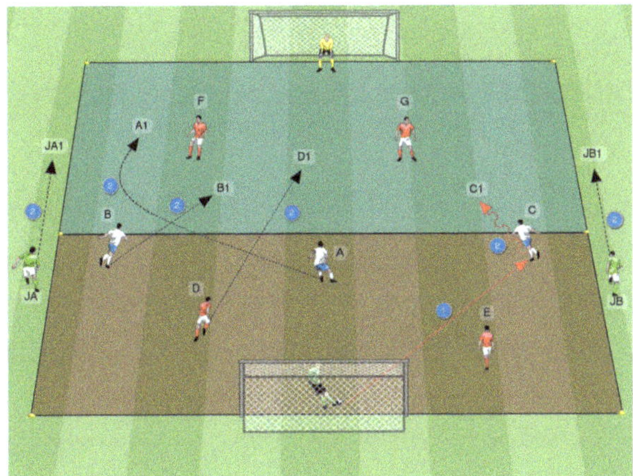

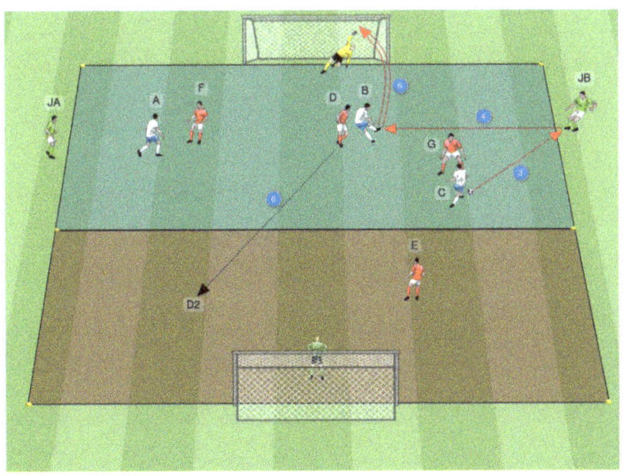

VARIATIONS

1. Touch limits.

2. Touch limits for the neutrals.

3. The goalkeepers can play with the defenders to keep possession.

COACHING POINTS	<ul><li>Encourage the players to finish with a shot on goal as quickly as possible.</li><li>In situations of momentary numerical inferiority, the defenders must mark the player with the ball and cover their teammate.</li><li>Avoid having the players position themselves on the same line, in order to guarantee balance when combining.</li><li>Always provide the player in possession with at least two passing options.</li><li>If the player in possession is in a "free ball" situation, the players without the ball should attack space in a pre-set manner.</li><li>After the player in possession releases the ball, they must move and make themselves available again.</li></ul>

3 VERSUS 4 WITH 1 INTERIOR NEUTRAL AND 2 EXTERIOR NEUTRALS

22

OPERATING METHOD Small-sided game

DURATION

14 minutes

OBJECTIVES

- Finishing
- Possession
- Width

EQUIPMENT	PREPARATION
- Cones to mark out the playing area - Seven bibs (four of one color and three of another) - Two goals - Balls	Playing area: 25-30 x 30-40 meters. Players: 10 + 2 goalkeepers. Number of series: Two of 5 minutes with 2 minutes of recuperation between series.

ORGANIZATION

In the space chosen for the activity use cones to set up the playing area. Place a goal on each end line. Divide the field into two equal halves, marking the midway point with poles. Divide the players into two teams; one team of four defenders (in red bibs, with two players positioned in each half) and one team of three attackers (in white shirts, who all start in the same zone). One neutral (in green bib) is located in the same zone as the attackers, while the other two neutral players (also in green bibs) start on separate wings. The goalkeepers occupy their respective goals. One of the goalkeepers initiates play by passing to an attacker, who attacks the opposite goal.

RULES

- The defenders may only leave their half of the field (one at a time) to help defend when the action is developing on the other side.
- After the sequence is finished or the ball is recovered, this player must quickly return to their zone.
- The attackers can score in either goal, except after receiving the ball from the goalkeeper at the start of play. In that situation, they must score in the opposite goal.
- The neutrals play with the team in possession.
- The external neutrals may only operate outside the playing area.
- If the defenders recover the ball and pass it to the goalkeeper, they earn a point.
- The attackers earn a point when they score a goal.
- Players change positions after every series.

In the example we see a possible passage of play, with a shot on goal by the white team after combining with the neutrals.

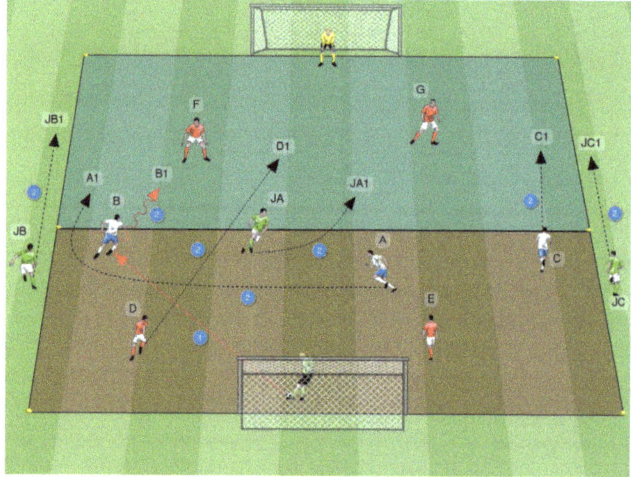

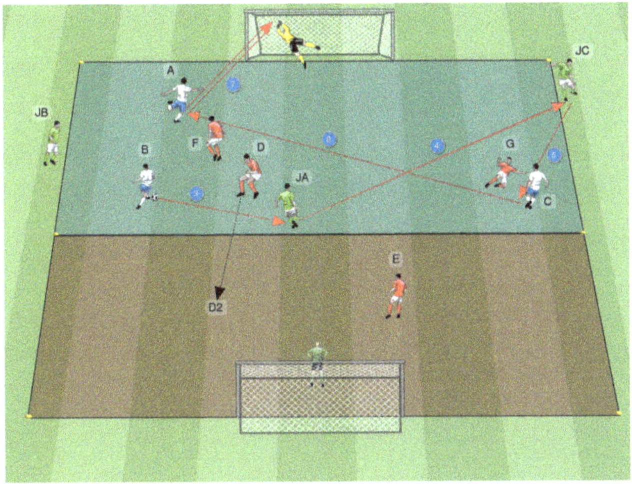

VARIATIONS

1. Touch limitations.

2. Touch limitations for the neutrals.

COACHING POINTS	<ul><li>The initial numerical superiority facilitates rapid finishing.</li><li>In situations of momentary numerical inferiority, the defenders must mark the player with the ball and cover their teammate.</li><li>Train the reaction to the defensive transition: the player closest to where the ball is lost should press the opponent while the teammates reduce the space.</li><li>Train the collective spacing of the players.</li><li>Avoid having the players position themselves on the same line, in order to guarantee balance when combining.</li><li>After the player in possession releases the ball, they must move and make themselves available again.</li></ul>

FROM 4 VERSUS 2 TO 4 VERSUS 4: RAPID VERTICAL PLAY

23

OPERATING METHOD Small-sided game

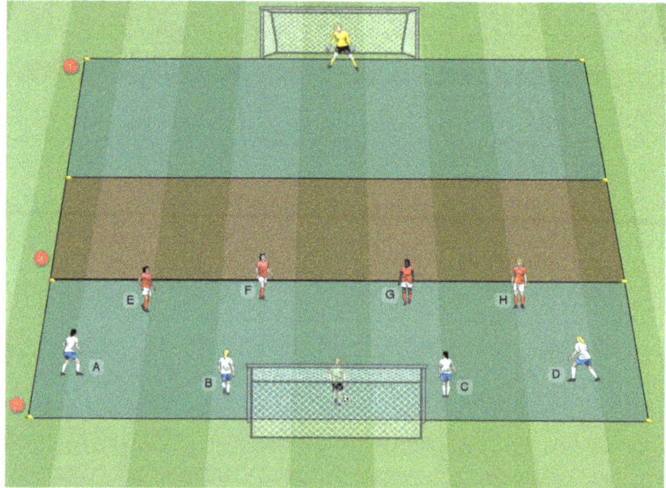

DURATION

14 minutes

OBJECTIVES

- Finishing
- Defending the goal

EQUIPMENT	PREPARATION
- Cones to mark out the playing area - Four bibs - Two goals - Balls	Playing area: 35-40 x 40-45 meters. Players: 8 + 2 goalkeepers. Number of series: Two of 5 minutes with 2 minutes of recuperation between series.

ORGANIZATION

In the space chosen for the activity set up the playing area and divide it into three horizontal zones; the two zones on the ends are of equal size and the central zone is narrower. Set up a goal on each end line. Divide the players into two teams of four (the defenders are in bibs and the attackers are in white shirts). All the players start in one lateral zone and the goalkeepers occupy their respective goals. One of the goalkeepers initiates play by passing to an attacker, who attacks the opposite goal.

RULES

- When the activity starts, two of the defenders detach from the play and retreat to the zone on the opposite end from the buildout.
- The remaining defenders have the task of slowing down the attack, up to the back edge of the central zone (Zone 3), allowing their teammates to retreat and take up positions near the goal.
- The attackers play in numerical superiority in the first two zones (4 versus 2), with the objective of reaching the opposite zone as quickly as possible in order to finish the play.
- The attackers can score in either goal, except after receiving the ball from the goalkeeper at the start of play. In that situation, they must score in the opposite goal.
- If the defenders win the ball, they must try to complete a pass to their goalkeeper. Every delivery to the netminder earns a point.
- Every goal scored by the attackers earns a point.
- The team that accumulates the most points in the two series wins.
- Players change positions after every series.

In the example we see a possible passage of play that ends with the attackers scoring a goal.

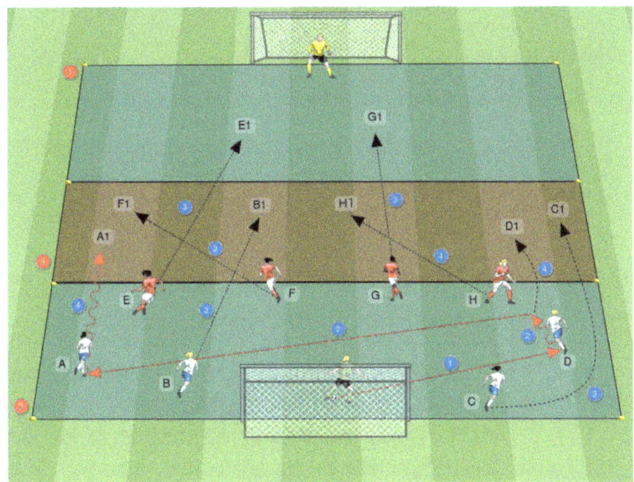

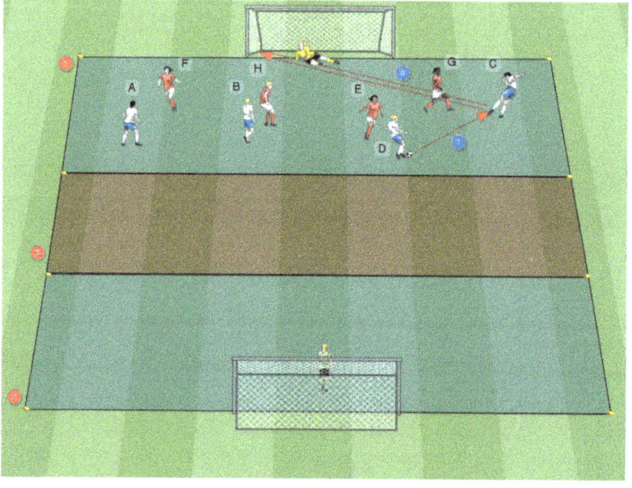

COACHING POINTS	<ul><li>Encourage the players to finish with a shot on goal as quickly as possible.</li><li>The attackers should look to play quickly in order to catch the attackers by surprise.</li><li>Encourage rapid repositioning by the defenders in response to the initial numerical inferiority.</li><li>In situations of momentary numerical inferiority, the defenders must mark the player with the ball and cover their teammate.</li></ul>

CREATING SPACE TO SHOOT

24

OPERATING METHOD Small-sided game

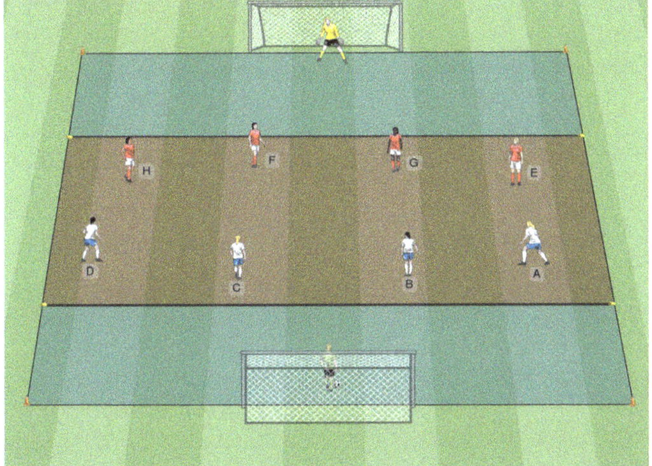

DURATION

24 minutes

OBJECTIVES

- **Penetration**
- **1 versus 1**
- **Finishing**
- **Shooting on goal**

EQUIPMENT	PREPARATION
<ul><li>**Eight cones**</li><li>**Four bibs**</li><li>**Two goals**</li><li>**Balls**</li></ul>	**Playing area: 35-40 x 40-45 meters.** **Players: 8/10/12 + 2 goalkeepers.** **Number of series: Three of 5 minutes with 3 minutes of recuperation between each series.**

ORGANIZATION

Set up the playing area in the space chosen for the activity with goals on each end line. In front of each goal, set up a zone ten meters deep, as shown in the illustration. Divide the players into two teams of four and position them within the central zone. The goalkeepers occupy their respective goals. One team starts with their goalkeeper in possession of the ball.

RULES

- Play using the normal rules of football.

- The players can only enter the attacking zones one at a time, and only by dribbling or by means of an interchange of passes.
- In the attacking zones, the players have three touches to finish the play.

In the example we see a possible passage of play that finishes with a goal for the white team after player C dribbles past player H.

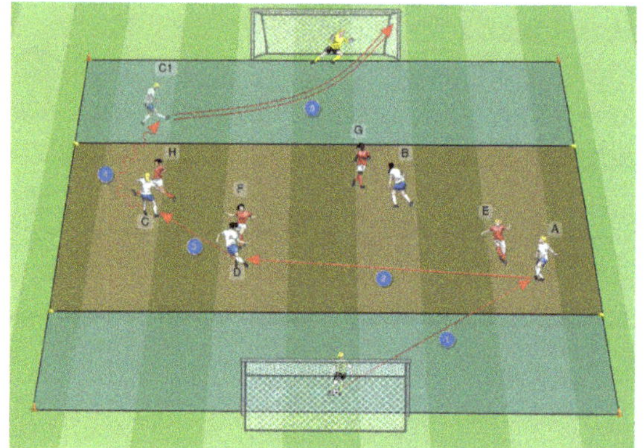

VARIATIONS

1. The players can enter the attacking zone two at a time.

2. Unlimited touches in the attacking zone.

3. Limit the type of passes allowed: in the central zone; only with hands, in the attacking zone; only with feet.

COACHING POINTS	- In possession:
	  - The arrangement of the players on the field allows for rapid changes of direction and a high speed of play, improving the aerobic capacity of the players.
	  - Encourage rapid, vertical play.
	  - Allow the players the freedom to take opponents on 1 versus 1.
	- Out of possession:
	  - Demand high pressure in order to recover the ball as quickly as possible.
	  - Balanced defending of the goal, according to collective tactical principles.
	  - Players prepared for attacking transitions.
	  - The goalkeeper gives verbal instructions to the defenders, and also takes up good positions in goal.

CREATING SPACE TO SHOOT WITH 2 NEUTRALS

25

OPERATING METHOD   Small-sided game

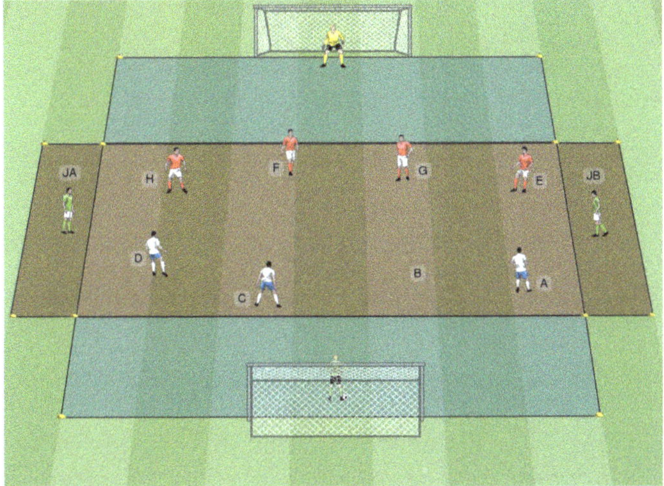

DURATION

24 minutes

OBJECTIVES

- Finishing
- 1 versus 1
- Shooting on goal
- Width
- Defensive cover

EQUIPMENT	PREPARATION
<ul><li>Twelve cones</li><li>Six bibs (four of one color and two of another)</li><li>Two goals</li><li>Balls</li></ul>	Playing area: 35-40 x 40-45 meters. Players: 8/10/12 + 2 goalkeepers. Number of series: Three of 5 minutes with 3 minutes of recuperation between each series.

ORGANIZATION

Set up the playing area in the space chosen for the activity, with goals on each end line. In front of each goal, set up a zone ten meters deep. On the sides of the central zone, set up two additional zones three meters wide, where the two neutrals are positioned (as shown in the illustration). Divide the players into two teams of four and position them within the central zone. The goalkeepers occupy their respective goals. One team starts with their goalkeeper in possession of the ball.

RULES

- Play using the normal rules of football.
- The neutrals play with the team in possession.
- The players can only enter the attacking zones one at a time, and only by dribbling or by means of an interchange of passes.
- In the attacking zones, the players have three touches to finish the play.

In the example we see a possible passage of play that finishes with a goal for the white team. After receiving a pass from a neutral, player C dribbles past player H.

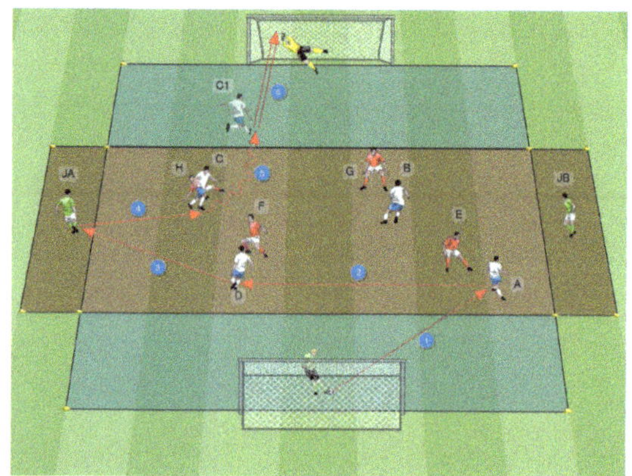

VARIATIONS

1. The players can enter the attacking zone two at a time.

2. Unlimited touches in the attacking zone.

3. Limit the type of passes allowed: in the central zone; only with hands, in the attacking zone; only with feet.

COACHING POINTS	<ul><li>In possession:<ul><li>The arrangement of the players on the field allows for rapid changes of direction and a high speed of play, improving the aerobic capacity of the players.</li><li>Encourage rapid, vertical play.</li><li>Allow the players the freedom to take opponents on 1 versus 1.</li></ul></li><li>Out of possession:<ul><li>Demand high pressure in order to recover the ball as quickly as possible.</li><li>Balanced defending of the goal, according to collective tactical principles.</li><li>Players prepared for attacking transitions.</li><li>The goalkeeper gives verbal instructions to the defenders, and also takes up good positions in goal.</li></ul></li></ul>

CREATING SPACE TO SHOOT WITH AN EXTERIOR TEAMMATE

26

OPERATING METHOD Small-sided game

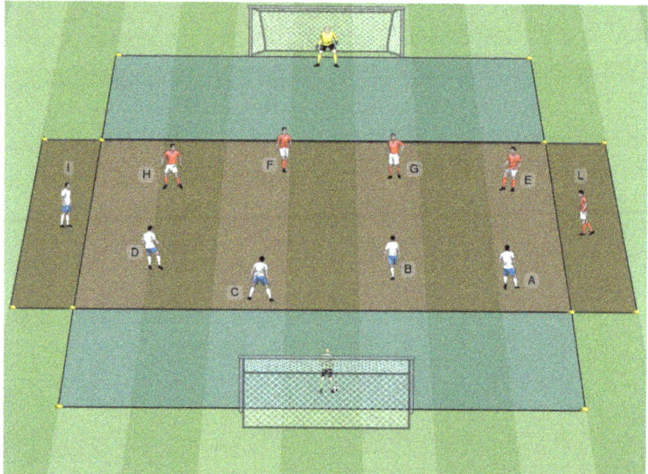

DURATION

24 minutes

OBJECTIVES

- **Finishing**
- **1 versus 1**
- **Shooting on goal**
- **Width**

EQUIPMENT

- **Twelve cones**
- **Five bibs**
- **Two goals**
- **Balls**

PREPARATION

Playing area: 35-40 x 40-45 meters.
Players: 8/10/12 + 2 goalkeepers.
Number of series: Three of 5 minutes with 3 minutes of recuperation between each series.

ORGANIZATION

Set up the playing area in the space chosen for the activity, with goals on each end line. In front of each goal, set up a zone ten meters deep. On the sides of the central zone, set up two additional zones three meters wide, where one player from each team will be positioned (as shown in the illustration). Divide the players into two teams of four and position them within the central zone. The goalkeepers occupy their respective goals. One team starts with their goalkeeper in possession of the ball.

RULES

- Play using the normal rules of football.
- The exterior players play with the team in possession.
- The players can only enter the attacking zones one at a time, and only by dribbling or by means of an interchange of passes.
- In the attacking zones, the players have three touches to finish the play.
- When an exterior teammate receives the ball from a player of the same color, they carry it into the playing area, while the interior teammate who made the pass takes their place on the outside.
- When an interior player passes to an exterior player of a different color, the receiver only plays a supporting role and remains in their position.

In the example we see a possible passage of play: after an interchange with a supporting player, the white team delivers the ball to the exterior white player, who enters the playing area and finishes the play after overcoming an opponent.

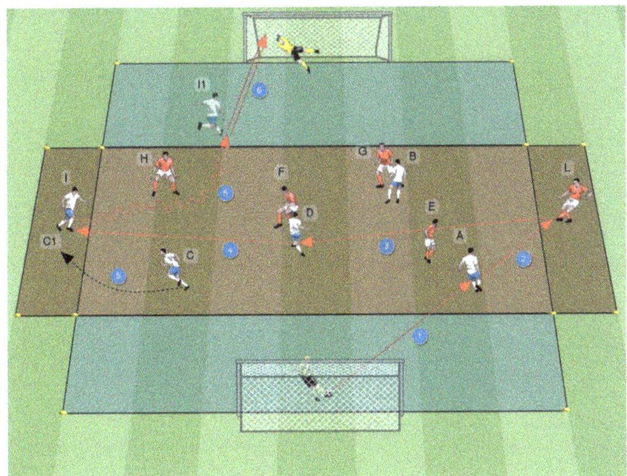

VARIATIONS

1. The players can enter the attacking zone two at a time.

2. Unlimited touches in the attacking zone.

3. Limit the type of passes allowed: in the central zone; only with hands, in the attacking zone; only with feet.

4. The outside player who enters the central zone can only enter the attacking zone only after an interchange.

COACHING POINTS	<ul><li>In possession:<ul><li>The arrangement of the players on the field allows for rapid changes of direction and a high speed of play, improving the aerobic capacity of the players.</li><li>Encourage rapid, vertical play.</li><li>Allow the players the freedom to take opponents on 1 versus 1.</li></ul></li><li>Out of possession:<ul><li>Demand high pressure in order to recover the ball as quickly as possible.</li><li>Players prepared for attacking transitions.</li><li>The goalkeeper gives verbal instructions to the defenders, and also takes up good positions in goal.</li></ul></li></ul>

4 VERSUS 4 + 2 EXTERIOR NEUTRALS

27

DURATION

14 minutes

OBJECTIVES

- Width
- Defending the goal
- Finishing
- Possession

EQUIPMENT

- Cones to mark out the playing area
- Six bibs (four of one color and two of another)
- Two goals
- Balls

PREPARATION

Playing area: 20-25 x 25-35 meters.
Players: 10 + 2 goalkeepers.
Number of series: Two of 5 minutes with 2 minutes of recuperation between series.

ORGANIZATION

Set up the playing area in the space chosen for the activity, with goals on each end line. Divide the players into two teams of four, who can position themselves freely within the playing area. One team can be seen in white shirts, and the other in red bibs. The two neutral players are positioned outside the playing area, one on each side. The goalkeepers occupy their respective goals. One of the goalkeepers initiates play by passing to a teammate who will attack the opposite goal.

RULES

- Each team attempts to score on their opponent's goal with the help of the exterior neutrals.
- The neutrals cannot enter the playing area (they are limited to supporting roles) and the interior players may not exchange positions with the neutrals.
- The neutrals play with the team in possession.
- Switch the neutral players from time to time.

In the example we see a possible passage of play that ends with a goal for the white team after combining with a neutral.

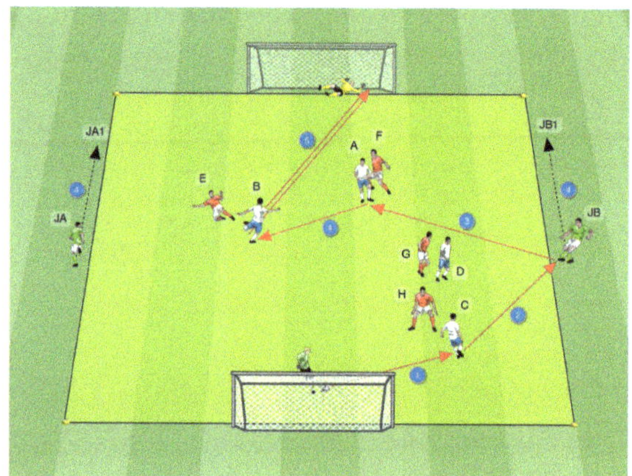

VARIATIONS

1. Touch limits.

2. Touch limits for the neutrals.

3. Require a combination with a neutral or a pre-established number of passes before scoring a goal.

COACHING POINTS	<ul><li>Encourage the players to finish with a shot on goal as quickly as possible.</li><li>Encourage the defenders to take up good positions to compensate for their numerical inferiority.</li><li>Train the collective spacing of the players.</li><li>Avoid having the players position themselves on the same line, in order to guarantee balance when combining.</li><li>Always provide the player in possession with at least two passing options.</li></ul>

4 VERSUS 4 + 2 EXTERIOR TEAMMATES

28

OPERATING METHOD Small-sided game

DURATION

14 minutes

OBJECTIVES

- **Width**
- **Finishing**
- **Defending the goal**
- **Possession**

EQUIPMENT

- **Cones to mark out the playing area**
- **Five bibs**
- **Two goals**
- **Balls**

PREPARATION

Playing area: 20-25 x 25-35 meters.
Players: 10 + 2 goalkeepers.
Number of series: Two of 5 minutes with 2 minutes of recuperation between series.

ORGANIZATION

Set up the playing area in the space chosen for the activity, with goals on each end line. Divide the players into two teams of five who can position themselves freely within the playing area, except for one player from each team who shall each be restricted to opposite sidelines. One team can be seen in white shirts, while the others are in red bibs. The goalkeepers occupy their respective goals. One of the goalkeepers initiates play by passing to a teammate who will attack the opposite goal.

RULES

- Each team attempts to score on their opponent's goal with the help of the exterior players.
- When an exterior teammate receives the ball from a player of the same color, they carry it into the playing area, while the interior teammate who made the pass takes their place on the outside.
- When an interior player passes to an exterior player of a different color, the receiver only plays a supporting role and remains in their position.

In the example we see a possible passage of play that ends with a goal for the white team after combining with the exterior teammates.

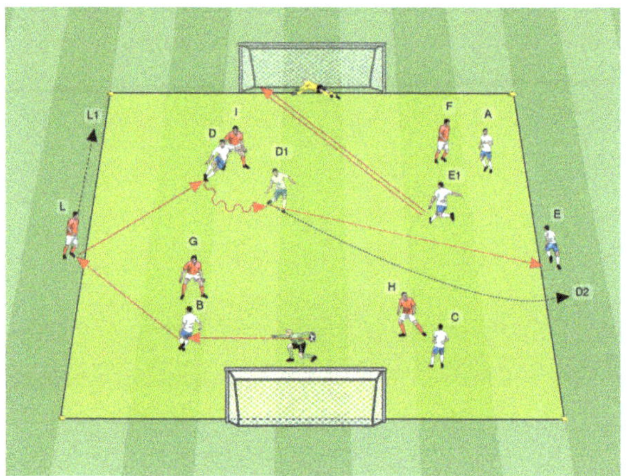

VARIATIONS

1. Touch limits.

2. Require a combination with an exterior player or a pre-established number of passes before scoring a goal.

COACHING POINTS	<ul><li>Encourage the players to finish with a shot on goal as quickly as possible.</li><li>The numerical superiority of the team in possession (thanks to the exterior players) facilitates rapid finishing on goal.</li><li>Encourage the defenders to take up good positions to compensate for their numerical inferiority.</li></ul>

4 VERSUS 4 + 2 INTERIOR NEUTRALS

29

OPERATING METHOD Small-sided game

DURATION

14 minutes

OBJECTIVES

- **Possession**
- **Shooting on goal**
- **Defending the goal**

EQUIPMENT

- **Cones to mark out the playing area**
- **Six bibs (four of one color and two of another)**
- **Two goals**
- **Balls**

PREPARATION

Playing area: 25-30 x 30-40 meters.
Players: 10 + 2 goalkeepers.
Number of series: Two of 5 minutes with 2 minutes of recuperation between series.

ORGANIZATION

Set up the playing area in the space chosen for the activity, with goals on each end line. Divide the players into two teams of four who can position themselves freely within the playing area. One team can be seen in white shirts, while the other is in red bibs. The two neutrals (in green bibs) are positioned inside the playing area. The goalkeepers occupy their respective goals. One of the goalkeepers initiates play by passing to a teammate who will attack the opposite goal.

RULES

- Each team attempts to score on their opponent's goal with the help of the neutrals who operate within the playing area.
- The neutrals play with the team in possession.
- Switch the neutral players from time to time.

In the example we see a possible passage of play that ends in a goal for the white team after they take advantage of the numerical superiority created by the neutral players.

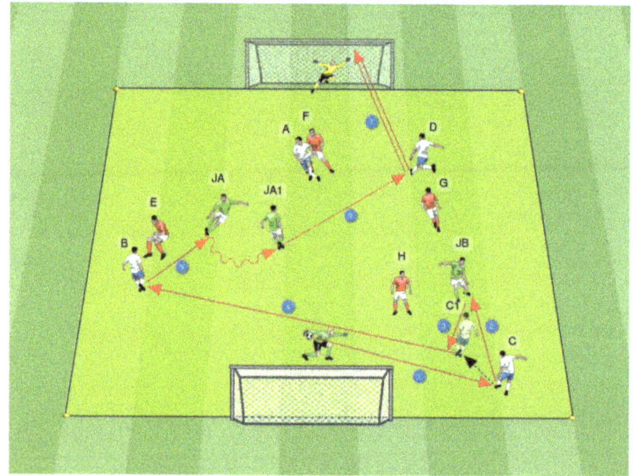

VARIATIONS

1. Touch limits.

2. Touch limits for the neutrals.

3. Require a combination with a neutral or a pre-established number of passes before scoring a goal.

COACHING POINTS	<ul><li>Encourage the players to finish with a shot on goal as quickly as possible.</li><li>Encourage the defenders to take up good positions to compensate for their numerical inferiority.</li><li>Train the reaction to the defensive transition: the player closest to where the ball is lost should press the opponent while the teammates reduce the space.</li><li>Always provide the player in possession with at least two passing options.</li><li>Train body orientation when receiving the ball. The players need to be profiled to face as much of the field as possible.</li></ul>

4 VERSUS 4 + 2 INTERIOR NEUTRALS AND 2 EXTERIOR NEUTRALS

30

OPERATING METHOD Small-sided game

DURATION

14 minutes

OBJECTIVES

- **Width**
- **Finishing**
- **Defending the goal**
- **Possession**

EQUIPMENT	PREPARATION
- **Cones to mark out the playing area** - **Eight bibs (four of one color and four of another)** - **Two goals** - **Balls**	**Playing area: 25-30 x 30-40 meters.** **Players: 12 + 2 goalkeepers.** **Number of series: Two of 5 minutes with 2 minutes of recuperation between series.**

ORGANIZATION

Set up the playing area in the space chosen for the activity, with goals on each end line. Divide the players into two teams of four who can position themselves freely within the playing area. One team can be seen in white shirts, while the other is in red bibs. The four neutrals are in green bibs. Two neutrals are positioned inside the playing area, while the other two are positioned beyond the playing area, one on each wing. The goalkeepers occupy their respective goals. One of the goalkeepers initiates play by passing to a teammate who will attack the opposite goal.

RULES

- Each team attempts to score on their opponent's goal with the help of the neutrals operating both inside and outside the playing area.
- The neutrals play with the team in possession.
- The interior neutrals (JA y JB) may not leave the playing area, while the exterior neutrals (JC y JD) may not enter the playing area.
- Switch the neutral players from time to time.

In the example we see a possible passage of play that ends in a goal for the white team, after they take advantage of the numerical superiority created by the interior neutral players and combining with the supporting exterior player.

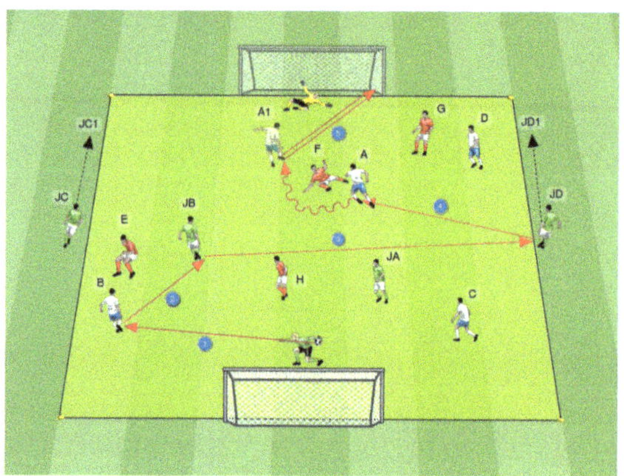

VARIATIONS

1. Touch limits.

2. Touch limits for the neutrals.

3. Require a combination with an exterior neutral or a pre-established number of passes before scoring a goal.

<table>
<tr>
<td>COACHING POINTS</td>
<td>

- Encourage the players to finish with a shot on goal as quickly as possible.
- The numerical superiority provided by the neutrals facilitates rapid finishing on goal.
- Encourage the defenders to take up good positions to compensate for their numerical inferiority.
- Always provide the player in possession with at least two passing options.
- Train body orientation when receiving the ball. The players need to be profiled to face as much of the field as possible.

</td>
</tr>
</table>

4 VERSUS 4 + 2 INTERIOR NEUTRALS AND 2 EXTERIOR TEAMMATES

31

OPERATING METHOD Small-sided game

DURATION

14 minutes

OBJECTIVES

- Width
- Finishing
- Possession

EQUIPMENT	PREPARATION
- Cones to mark out the playing area - Seven bibs (five of one color and two of another) - Two goals - Balls	Playing area: 25-30 x 30-40 meters. Players: 12 + 2 goalkeepers. Number of series: Two of 5 minutes with 2 minutes of recuperation between series.

ORGANIZATION

Set up the playing area in the space chosen for the activity, with goals on each end line. Divide the players into two teams of five, who can position themselves freely within the playing area, except for one player from each team who shall each be restricted to opposite sidelines. One team can be seen in white shirts, while the other is in red bibs. The two neutrals are in green bibs and are positioned inside the playing area. The goalkeepers occupy their respective goals. One of the goalkeepers initiates play by passing to a teammate who will attack the opposite goal.

RULES

- Each team attempts to score on their opponent's goal with the help of the neutrals operating inside and the supporting players operating outside the playing area.
- When an exterior teammate receives the ball from a player of the same color, they carry it into the playing area, while the interior teammate who made the pass takes their place on the outside.
- When an interior player passes to an exterior player of a different color, the receiver only plays a supporting role and remains in their position.
- The neutrals cannot leave the playing area.
- The neutrals play with the team that passes them the ball.
- Switch the neutral players from time to time.

In the example we see a possible passage of play that ends in a goal for the white team after they take advantage of the numerical superiority created by the interior neutrals and exterior players.

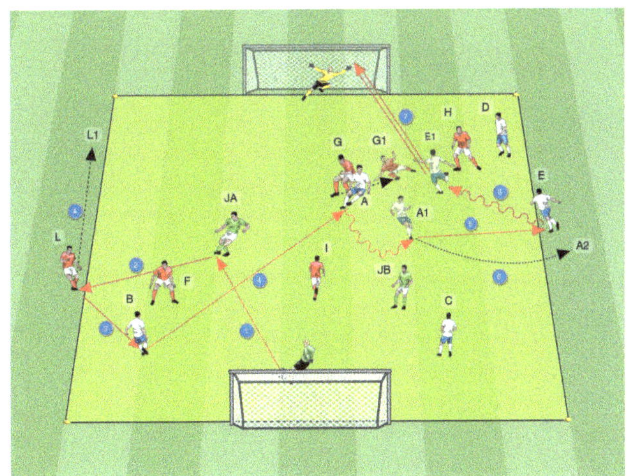

VARIATIONS

1. Touch limits.

2. Touch limits for the neutrals.

3. Require a combination with an exterior player and interior neutral or a pre-established number of passes before scoring a goal.

<table>
<tr><td>COACHING POINTS</td><td>

- Encourage the players to finish with a shot on goal as quickly as possible.
- The numerical superiority provided by the outside players and interior neutrals facilitates rapid finishing on goal.
- Encourage the defenders to take up good positions to compensate for their numerical inferiority.

</td></tr>
</table>

4 VERSUS 4 VERSUS 4: POSSESSION IN ZONES

32

OPERATING METHOD Small-sided game

DURATION

12minutes

OBJECTIVES

- **Transitions**
- **Possession**
- **Dismarking**
- **Passing**

EQUIPMENT

- **Cones to mark out the playing area**
- **Eight bibs (four of one color and four of another)**
- **Balls**

PREPARATION

Playing area: 50 x 70 meters.
Players: 12 + 2 goalkeepers.
Number of series: Two of 4 minutes with 2 minutes of recuperation between series.

ORGANIZATION

In the space chosen for the activity set up a 50x70 meter field and use the cones to divide it into 5 zones, in this order: 10 meters (Goalkeeper Zone), 20 meters (Zone One), 10 meters (Neutral Zone), 20 meters (Zone Two), and 10 meters (Goalkeeper Zone). Divide the players into three teams of four, with two teams occupying Zone One and the third occupying Zone Two. The goalkeepers occupy the zones on each end. One goalkeeper initiates play by passing to one of the teams in Zone One.

RULES

- The white team plays against the red team and tries to maintain possession in Zone One while looking for a passing line that will allow the ball to be delivered to Zone Two.
- Once the ball is delivered to Zone Two, the white team follows and defends against the yellow team, who must maintain possession in order to create space and find a way to connect to the team that has remained in Zone One.
- The goalkeepers offer support and play with their feet.
- The ball cannot be played from inside the neutral area.
- If the defenders win the ball, the teams switch roles, with the defenders becoming the attackers and the attackers becoming the defenders.
- Play always restarts from a goalkeeper.
- The activity is continuous: If the ball leaves the playing area, restart play with the goalkeeper.

In the example we see a possible passage of play. After the White team finds space to pass to the yellow team in zone two, the yellow keeps possession with the help of the goalkeeper and then creates space to connect with the red team in Zone One.

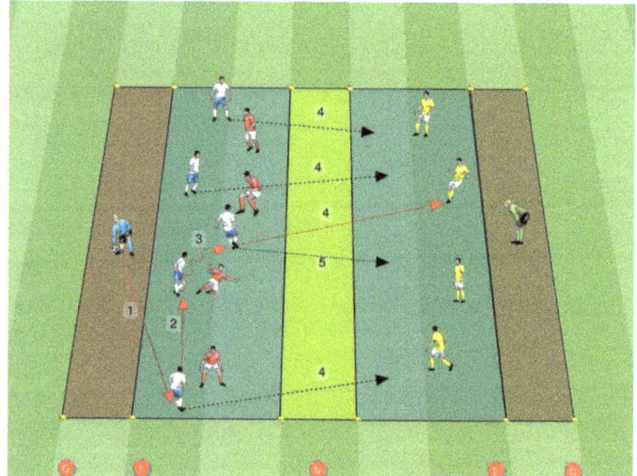

VARIATIONS

1. Require a minimum number of passes before allowing the ball to be delivered to the team in the other zone.

COACHING POINTS	<ul><li>Train the reaction to the defensive transition: the player closest to where the ball is lost should press the opponent while the teammates reduce the space.</li><li>Train the proper spacing of all the players.</li><li>Avoid having the players position themselves on the same line, in order to guarantee balance when combining.</li><li>Always provide the player in possession with at least two passing options.</li><li>Train body orientation when receiving the ball. The players need to be profiled to face as much of the field as possible.</li></ul>

4 VERSUS 4 VERSUS 4 + 2 NEUTRALS: POSSESSION IN ZONES

33

OPERATING METHOD Small-sided game

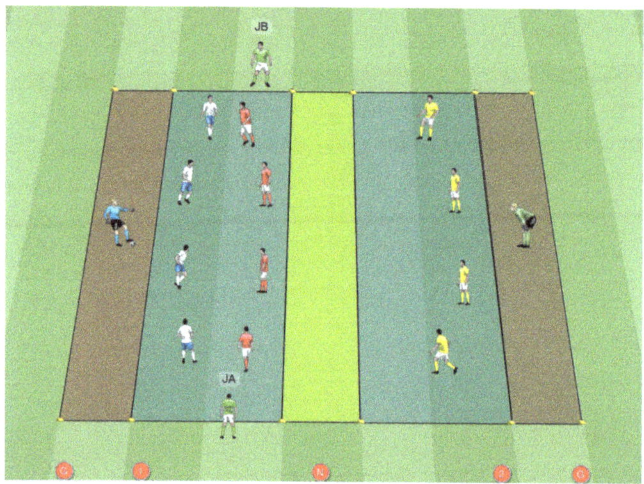

DURATION

12 minutes

OBJECTIVES

- Transitions
- Width
- Possession
- Passing

EQUIPMENT

- Cones to mark out the playing area
- Ten bibs (four reds, four yellows and two greens)
- Balls

PREPARATION

Playing area: 50 x 70 meters.
Players: 14 + 2 goalkeepers.
Number of series: Two of 4 minutes with 2 minutes of recuperation between series.

ORGANIZATION

In the space chosen for the activity set up a 50x70 meter field and use the cones to divide it into 5 zones, in this order: 10 meters (Goalkeeper Zone), 20 meters (Zone One), 10 meters (Neutral Zone), 20 meters (Zone Two), and 10 meters (Goalkeeper Zone). Divide the players into three teams of four, with two teams occupying Zone One and the third occupying Zone Two. Two neutral players operate along the length of the wing; one on each side. The goalkeepers occupy the zones on each end. One goalkeeper initiates play, passing to one of the teams in Zone One.

RULES

- The white team plays against the red team and tries to maintain possession in Zone One while looking for a passing line that will allow the ball to be delivered to Zone Two.
- Once the ball is delivered to Zone Two, the white team follows and defends against the yellow team, who must maintain possession in order to create space and find a way to connect to the team that has remained in Zone One.
- The goalkeepers offer support and play with their feet.
- The ball cannot be played from inside the neutral area.
- If the defenders win the ball, the teams switch roles, with the defenders becoming the attackers and the attackers becoming the defenders.
- The team in possession can combine with the neutral players.
- The neutrals cannot enter the field and must operate from outside the playing area.
- Play always restarts from a goalkeeper.
- The activity is continuous: if the ball leaves the playing area, restart play with the goalkeeper.

In the example we see a possible passage of play. With help from one of the neutrals, the white team finds space to pass to the yellow team in Zone Two. The yellow team keeps possession with the help of the goalkeeper (and the other neutral) and then creates space to connect with the red team in Zone One.

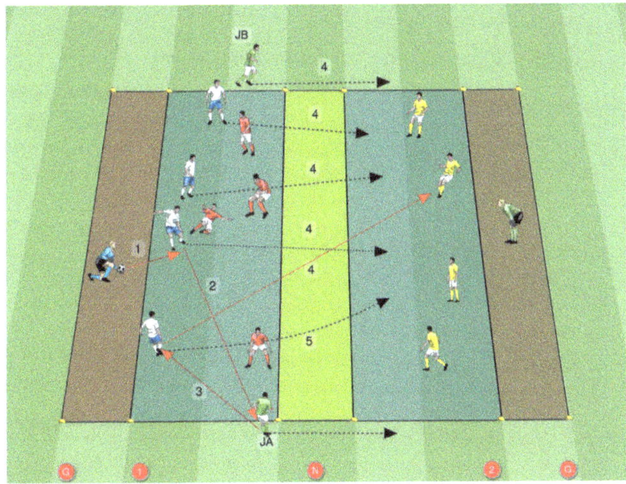

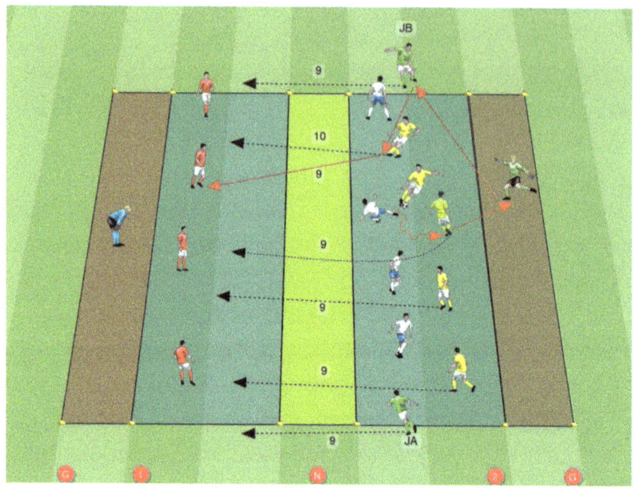

VARIATIONS

1. Touch limits for the neutrals.

2. Require a minimum number of passes before allowing the ball to be delivered to the team in the other zone.

<table>
<tr><td rowspan="2">COACHING POINTS</td><td>• Always provide the player in possession with at least two passing options.</td></tr>
<tr><td>• Train body orientation when receiving the ball. The players need to be profiled to face as much of the field as possible.</td></tr>
</table>

SCORE AFTER COMBINATION PLAY

34

OPERATING METHOD   Small-sided game

DURATION

20 minutes

OBJECTIVES

- **Finishing**
- **Wall pass**
- **Shooting on goal**

EQUIPMENT

- **Four cones**
- **Six bibs**
- **Two goals**
- **Ten balls**

PREPARATION

Playing area: 25-35 x 35-45 meters.
Players: 8/10/12 + 2 goalkeepers.
Number of series: Two of 6 minutes with 4 minutes of recuperation between series.

ORGANIZATION

In the space chosen for the activity use the cones to set up the playing area. Set up goals on both end lines. Divide the players into two teams of six players, with the goalkeepers in their respective goals. Spread out ten balls within the playing area.

RULES

- On the coach's signal, the players can choose a ball and try to score.
- A team can attack with more than one ball, but only on one goal at a time.
- The two teams can attack and defend at the same time with different players.
- The two teams can only score after a combination play between their players.

In the example we see a possible passage of play that ends with goals for both the red and the white teams.

COACHING POINTS	<ul><li>In possession:</li><li>Allow the players freedom of action in order to stimulate personal initiative.</li><li>Out of possession:<ul><li>Defend the goal.</li><li>Take up good positions.</li><li>Block the paths to goal.</li></ul></li></ul>

6 VERSUS 6 OVERCOMING THE MIDFIELD LINE

35

OPERATING METHOD Small-sided game

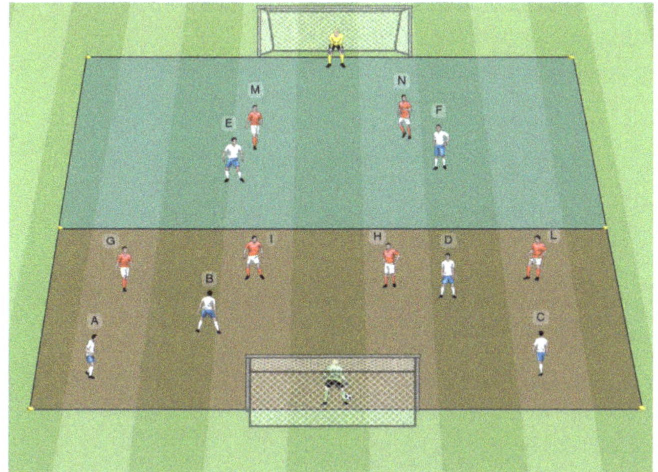

DURATION

14 minutes

OBJECTIVES

- Possession
- Finishing

EQUIPMENT	PREPARATION
<ul><li>Cones to mark out the playing area</li><li>Six bibs</li><li>Two goals</li><li>Balls</li></ul>	Playing area: 25-35 x 35-45 meters. Players: 12 + 2 goalkeepers. Number of series: Two of 5 minutes with 2 minutes of recuperation between series.

ORGANIZATION

In the space chosen for the activity set up a playing area using the cones and divide it into two equal parts. Set up goals on both end lines. Divide the players into two teams of six (one team can be seen in white and the other wears red bibs), who may move freely within the playing area. The goalkeepers occupy their respective goals. One of the goalkeepers initiates play by passing to a teammate who will attack the opposite goal.

RULES

- Each team attempts to score in their opponent's goal. Goals are only valid if, at the moment of finishing, the entire attacking team is in the opponent's half of the field.
- At the same time, the defending team must also try to retreat to their half of the field before the goal is scored. If they don't, then the goal counts double.

In the example we see a possible passage of play that ends with a goal for the white team that is worth one point, because the players from both teams had crossed over the midfield line before the goal was scored.

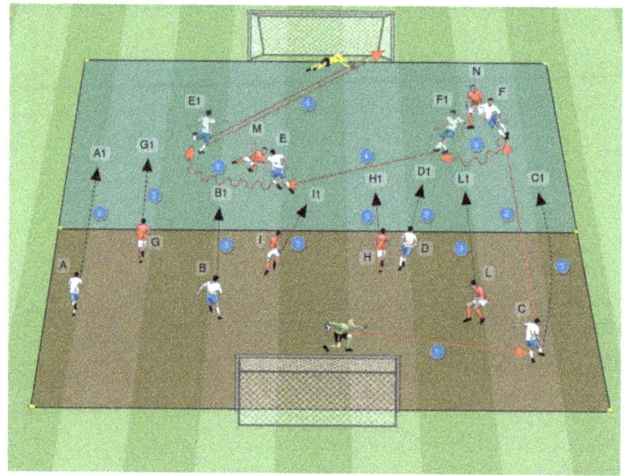

VARIATIONS

1. Touch limits.

2. Require a combination or a pre-established number of passes before a goal can be scored.

COACHING POINTS	<ul><li>Encourage the attacking players to finish with a shot on goal as quickly as possible.</li><li>Encourage the players out of possession to take up good positions and work as a unit in the defensive phase.</li></ul>

6 VERSUS 6 + 2 EXTERIOR NEUTRALS: OVERCOMING THE MIDFIELD LINE

36

OPERATING METHOD Small-sided game

DURATION

14 minutes

OBJECTIVES

- Shooting on goal
- Defending the goal
- Transitions

EQUIPMENT	PREPARATION
<ul><li>Cones to mark out the playing area</li><li>Eight bibs (six of one color and two of another)</li><li>Two goals</li><li>Balls</li></ul>	Playing area: 25-35 x 35-45 meters. Players: 14 + 2 goalkeepers. Number of series: Two of 5 minutes with 2 minutes of recuperation between series.

ORGANIZATION

In the space chosen for the activity use the cones to set up the playing area and divide it into two equal parts. Set up goals on both end lines. Divide the players into two teams of six (one can be seen in white and the other wears red bibs), who may move freely within the playing area. The two neutral players (in green bibs) are located outside the playing area; one on each side. The goalkeepers occupy their respective goals. One of the goalkeepers initiates play by passing to a teammate who will attack the opposite goal.

RULES

- Each team attempts to score in their opponent's goal. Goals are only valid if, at the moment of finishing, the entire attacking team is in the opponent's half of the field.
- At the same time, the defending team must also try to retreat to their half of the field before the goal is scored. If they don't, then the goal counts double.
- The neutrals may not enter the playing area and can only act as supporting players.
- The neutrals play with the team in possession.
- The interior players may not mark the neutral players.

In the example we see a possible passage of play that ends with a goal for the white team that is worth one point, because the players from both teams had crossed over the midfield line before the goal was scored.

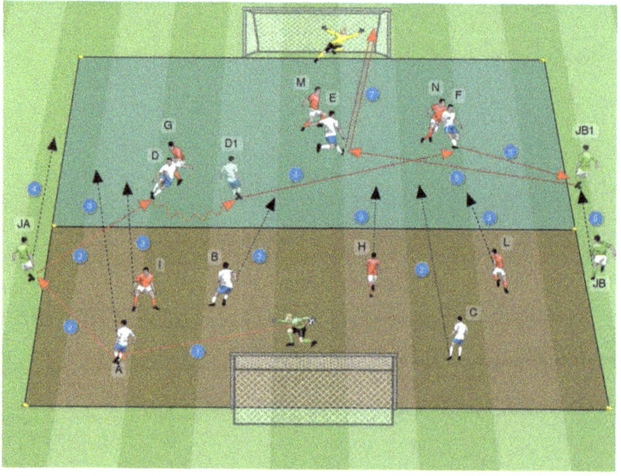

VARIATIONS

1. Touch limits.

2. Touch limits for the neutrals.

3. Require a combination with a supporting player or a pre-established number of passes before a goal can be scored.

COACHING POINTS	<ul><li>Encourage the attacking players to finish with a shot on goal as quickly as possible.</li><li>The initial numerical superiority facilitates rapid finishing.</li><li>In situations of momentary numerical inferiority, the defenders must mark the player with the ball and cover their teammate.</li><li>After the player in possession releases the ball, they must move and make themselves available again.</li></ul>

6 VERSUS 6: SCORE IN THE LARGE GOAL OR THE TWO MINI-GOALS OUT WIDE

37

OPERATING METHOD Small-sided game

DURATION

14 minutes

OBJECTIVES

- Width
- Shooting on goal
- Defending the goal
- Switching play

EQUIPMENT

- Cones to mark out the playing area
- Six bibs
- Two goals
- Eight tall cones
- Balls

PREPARATION

Playing area: 25-35 x 35-45 meters.
Players: 12 + 2 goalkeepers.
Number of series: Two of 5 minutes with 2 minutes of recuperation between series.

ORGANIZATION

In the space chosen for the activity use the cones to set up the playing area. Set up a regulation size goal on each end line. In the four corners of the field, use the tall cones to create four mini-goals, each about two meters wide (as shown in the illustration). Divide the players into two teams of six (one is seen in white and the other in red bibs), who may move freely about the playing area. Two goalkeepers occupy their respective goals. One of the goalkeepers initiates play by passing to a teammate who will attack the opposite goal.

RULES

- Each team attempts to score in the opponent's large goal or two mini-goals.
- Teams can only score in the regulation sized goal by means of a header or a volley out of the air, but they can score on the mini-goals in any manner.

In the examples we see one possible passage of play that ends with a headed goal in the large goal and another that concludes with a finish in one of the mini-goals.

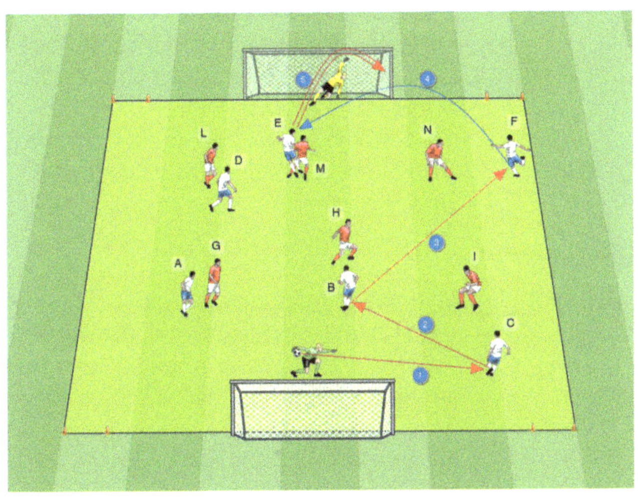

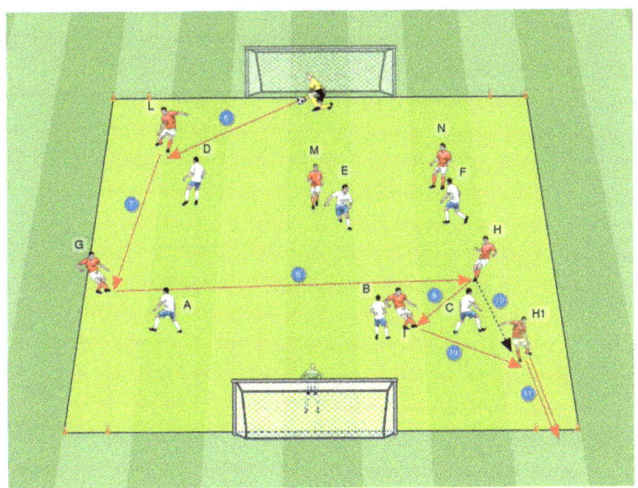

VARIATIONS

1. Touch limits.

2. Require a pre-established number of passes before a goal can be scored.

COACHING POINTS	<ul><li>Encourage the attacking players to finish with a shot on goal as quickly as possible.</li><li>The initial numerical superiority facilitates rapid finishing.</li><li>In situations of momentary numerical inferiority, the defenders must mark the player with the ball and cover their teammate.</li><li>Train the reaction to the defensive transition: the player closest to where the ball is lost should press the opponent while the teammates reduce the space.</li><li>Train the collective spacing of the players.</li><li>Avoid having the players position themselves on the same line, in order to ensure balance when combining.</li><li>Always provide the player in possession with at least two passing options.</li><li>After the player in possession releases the ball, they must move and make themselves available again.</li></ul>

6 VERSUS 6: GOAL ONLY VALID AFTER PLAYING THROUGH A MINI-GOAL

38

OPERATING METHOD Small-sided game

DURATION

14 minutes

OBJECTIVES

- **Finishing**
- **Running with the ball**
- **Dribbling**
- **Possession**

EQUIPMENT	PREPARATION
<ul><li>**Cones to mark out the playing area**</li><li>**Six bibs**</li><li>**Two goals**</li><li>**Eight tall cones**</li><li>**Balls**</li></ul>	**Playing area: 25-35 x 35-45 meters.** **Players: 12 + 2 goalkeepers.** **Number of series: Two of 5 minutes with 2 minutes of recuperation between series.**

ORGANIZATION

In the space chosen for the activity use the cones to set up the playing area. Set up a regulation size goal on each end line. Use the tall cones to create four mini-goals, each about one and a half meters wide (as shown in the illustration) and all at the same distance from the large goals (as shown in the illustration). Divide the players into two teams of six, who may move freely about the playing area. Two goalkeepers occupy their respective goals. One of the goalkeepers initiates play by passing to a teammate who will attack the opposite goal.

RULES

- Each team attacks one goal and defends the other.
- Before a team can score, one of their players must run with the ball through one of the mini-goals (in either direction).
- Each goal scored is worth one point.
- Play is continuous. When a goal is scored, the goalkeeper of the team that was scored on restarts play.

In the example we see a possible passage of play, with the white team scoring a goal after dribbling through one of the mini-goals.

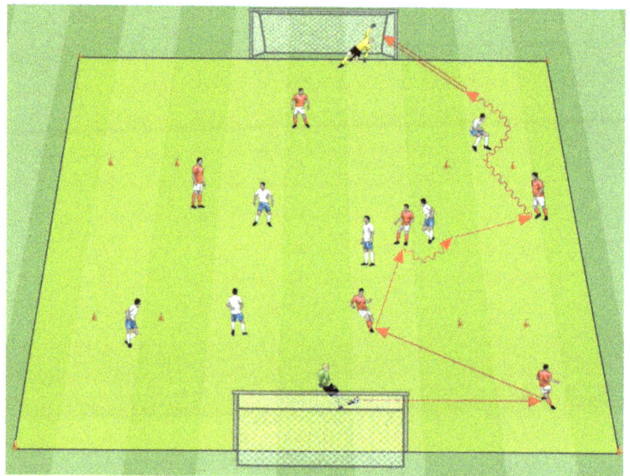

VARIATIONS

1. Touch limits.

COACHING POINTS

- Train the reaction to the defensive transition: the player closest to where the ball is lost should press the opponent while the teammates reduce the space.
- If the player in possession is in a "free ball" situation, the players without the ball should attack space in a pre-set manner.
- After the player in possession releases the ball, they must move and make themselves available again.
- To ensure continuous movement and to maintain appropriate depth, two nearby players who find themselves on the same line should move to create diagonal lines of support.

6 VERSUS 6 + 2 NEUTRALS: GOAL ONLY VALID AFTER PLAYING THROUGH A MINI-GOAL

39

OPERATING METHOD Small-sided game

DURATION

14 minutes

OBJECTIVES

- Finishing
- Shooting on goal
- Defending the goal
- Possession

EQUIPMENT	PREPARATION
<ul><li>Cones to mark out the playing area</li><li>Eight bibs (six of one color and two of another)</li><li>Two goals</li><li>Eight tall cones</li><li>Balls</li></ul>	Playing area: 25-35 x 35-45 meters. Players: 14 + 2 goalkeepers. Number of series: Two of 5 minutes with 2 minutes of recuperation between series.

ORGANIZATION

In the space chosen for the activity use the cones to set up the playing area. Set up a regulation size goal on each end line. Use the tall cones to create four mini-goals, each about one and a half meters wide (as shown in the illustration) and all at the same distance from the large goals (as shown in the illustration). Divide the players into two teams of six, who may move freely about the playing area. Position two neutral players (in green bibs) outside the playing area; one on each side. Two

goalkeepers occupy their respective goals. One of the goalkeepers initiates play by passing to a teammate who will attack the opposite goal.

RULES

- Each team attacks one goal and defends the other.
- Before a team can score, one of their players must run with the ball through one of the small goals (in either direction).
- Each goal scored is worth one point.
- The neutrals can only offer support and may not enter the playing area.
- Play is continuous. When a goal is scored, the goalkeeper of the team that was scored on restarts play.

In the example we see a possible passage of play, with the white team scoring a goal after utilizing a neutral and dribbling through one of the mini-goals.

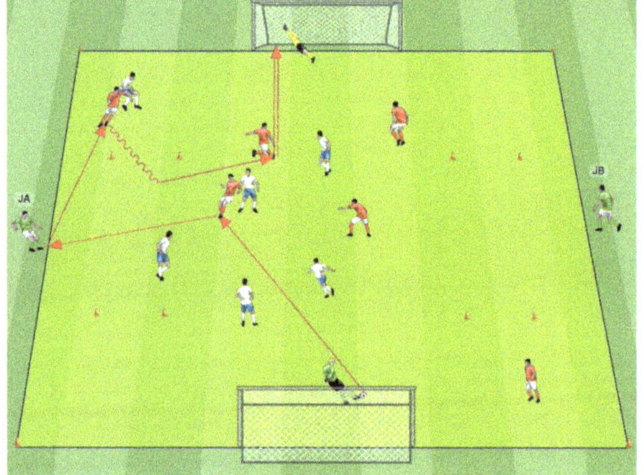

VARIATIONS

1. Touch limits.

2. Touch limits for the neutrals.

COACHING POINTS	- Encourage the players to finish with a shot on goal as quickly as possible. - Encourage the players to move the ball to a new area as soon as they go through a mini-goal. - Encourage the defenders to first cover the mini-goals and then quickly move to defend the large goal. - Encourage the use of the neutrals in order to take advantage of the numerical superiority. - Train the collective spacing of the players. - Always provide the player in possession with at least two passing options.

6 VERSUS 6 + EXTERNAL TEAMMATES

40

 Small-sided game

DURATION

14 minutes

OBJECTIVES

- **Finishing**
- **Shooting on goal**
- **Defending the goal**
- **Possession**

EQUIPMENT

- **Cones to mark out the playing area**
- **Six bibs**
- **Two goals**
- **Eight tall cones**
- **Balls**

PREPARATION

Playing area: 25-35 x 35-45 meters.
Players: 14 + 2 goalkeepers.
Number of series: Two of 5 minutes with 2 minutes of recuperation between series.

ORGANIZATION

In the space chosen for the activity use the cones to set up the playing area. Set up a regulation size goal on each end line. Use the tall cones to create four mini-goals, each about one and a half meters wide (as shown in the illustration) and all at the same distance from the large goals (as shown in the illustration). Divide the players into two teams of seven, who may move freely about the playing area, except for one player from each team who shall each be restricted to opposite sidelines. Two goalkeepers occupy their respective goals. One of the goalkeepers initiates play by passing to a teammate who will attack the opposite goal.

RULES

- Each team attacks one goal and defends the other.
- Before a team can score, one of their players must run with the ball through one of the small goals (in either direction).
- Each goal scored is worth one point.
- When an interior player passes to an exterior player of the same color, the receiver carries the ball into the playing area, while the passer replaces them on the outside.
- When an interior player passes to an exterior player of a different color, the receiver only plays a supporting role and remains in their position.
- Play is continuous. When a goal is scored, the goalkeeper of the team that was scored on restarts play.

In the example we see a possible passage of play, with the white team scoring a goal after utilizing the outside players and dribbling through one of the mini-goals.

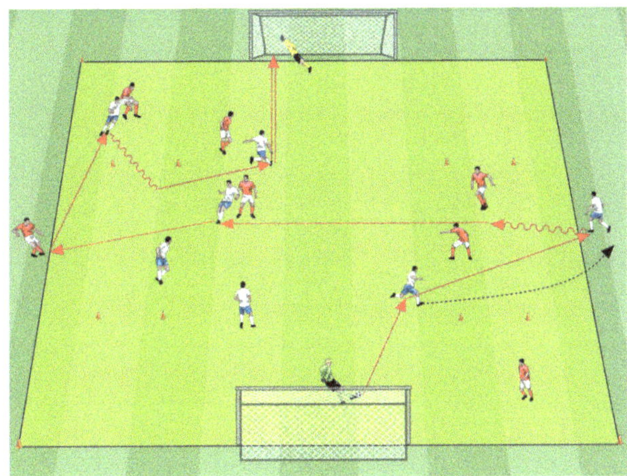

VARIATIONS

1. Touch limits.

2. Touch limits for the exterior players.

3. Require a pass to an exterior player before scoring.

COACHING POINTS	<ul><li>Encourage the players to move the ball to a new area as soon as they go through a mini-goal.</li><li>Encourage the defenders to first cover the mini-goals and then quickly move to defend the large goal.</li><li>Encourage the use of the exterior players in order to take advantage of the numerical superiority.</li></ul>

6 VERSUS 6: RESTRICTED ZONE

41

OPERATING METHOD Small-sided game

DURATION

14 minutes

OBJECTIVES

- Width
- Shooting on goal
- Defending the goal
- Possession
- Switching play

EQUIPMENT	PREPARATION
- Cones to mark out the playing area - Six bibs - Two goals - Balls	Playing area: 25-35 x 35-45 meters. Players: 12 + 2 goalkeepers. Number of series: Two of 5 minutes with 2 minutes of recuperation between series.

ORGANIZATION

In the space chosen for the activity use the cones to set up the playing area. Set up a regulation size goal on each end line. In the middle of the field, set up a 10x8 meter rectangle. Divide the players into two teams of six, who may move freely about the playing area. Two goalkeepers occupy their respective goals. One of the goalkeepers initiates play by passing to a teammate who will attack the opposite goal.

RULES

- The ball may not enter the central rectangle.

- Each team attacks one goal and defends the other.
- Each goal scored is worth one point.
- Play is continuous. When a goal is scored, the goalkeeper of the team that was scored on restarts play.

In the example we see a possible passage of play, with the white team scoring a goal.

VARIATIONS

1. Touch limits.

2. The players may not enter the rectangle.

3. Vary the dimensions of the rectangle to adjust the difficulty level of the activity.

COACHING POINTS	<ul><li>Encourage the players to finish with a shot on goal as quickly as possible.</li><li>Play must be developed through the wings.</li><li>Train the reaction to the defensive transition: the player closest to where the ball is lost should press the opponent while the teammates reduce the space.</li><li>Train the collective spacing of the players.</li><li>Avoid having the players position themselves on the same line, in order to guarantee balance when combining.</li><li>Always provide the player in possession with at least two passing options.</li></ul>

6 VERSUS 6 WITH A NEUTRAL IN THE RESTRICTED ZONE

42

OPERATING METHOD Small-sided game

DURATION

14 minutes

OBJECTIVES

- Width
- Shooting on goal
- Defending the goal
- Possession
- Switching play

EQUIPMENT	PREPARATION
<ul><li>Cones to mark out the playing area</li><li>Seven bibs (six of one color and one of another)</li><li>Two goals</li><li>Balls</li></ul>	Playing area: 25-35 x 35-45 meters. Players: 13 + 2 goalkeepers. Number of series: Two of 5 minutes with 2 minutes of recuperation between series.

ORGANIZATION

In the space chosen for the activity use the cones to set up the playing area. Set up a regulation size goal on each end line. In the middle of the field, set up a 10x8 meter rectangle. Divide the players into two teams of six, who may move freely about the playing area. One neutral, who plays with the team in possession, is positioned inside the central rectangle. Two goalkeepers occupy their respective goals. One of the goalkeepers initiates play by passing to a teammate who will attack the opposite

goal.

RULES

- The ball may not enter the central rectangle unless it is to combine with the neutral player, who returns it to the team in possession.
- The defending team cannot obstruct the neutral.
- The neutral cannot leave the rectangle.
- Each team attacks one goal and defends the other.
- Each goal scored is worth one point.
- Play is continuous. When a goal is scored, the goalkeeper of the team that was scored on restarts play.

In the example we see a possible passage of play, with the white team scoring a goal with the help of the neutral player.

VARIATIONS

1. Touch limits.

2. Touch limits for the neutral.

3. The players may enter the rectangle.

4. Vary the dimensions of the rectangle to adjust the difficulty level of the activity.

<table>
<tr>
<td>COACHING POINTS</td>
<td>

- Encourage the players to finish with a shot on goal as quickly as possible.
- Encourage the team out of possession to defend all areas of the field.
- Play must be developed through the wings.
- Encourage the players to keep possession until they can find the best options for finishing the action.
- Encourage the players to look for the neutral in order to create a numerical superiority.

</td>
</tr>
</table>

6 VERSUS 6: RESTRICTED ZONE WITH EXTERIOR NEUTRALS

43

OPERATING METHOD Small-sided game

DURATION

14 minutes

OBJECTIVES

- Width
- Shooting on goal
- Defending the goal
- Switching play
- Possession

EQUIPMENT

- Cones to mark out the playing area
- Eight bibs (six of one color and two of another)
- Two goals
- Balls

PREPARATION

Playing area: 25-35 x 35-45 meters.
Players: 14 + 2 goalkeepers.
Number of series: Two of 5 minutes with 2 minutes of recuperation between series.

ORGANIZATION

In the space chosen for the activity use the cones to set up the playing area. Set up a regulation size goal on each end line. In the middle of the field, set up a 10x8 meter rectangle. Divide the players into two teams of six, who may move freely about the playing area. Two neutrals operate on the wings outside the playing area and play with the team in possession. Two goalkeepers occupy their respective goals. One of the goalkeepers initiates play by passing to a teammate who will attack the opposite goal.

RULES

- The ball may not enter the central rectangle.
- The players cannot obstruct the neutrals.
- The neutrals offer wide support for the team in possession of the ball.
- Each team attacks one goal and defends the other.
- Each goal scored is worth one point.
- Play is continuous. When a goal is scored, the goalkeeper of the team that was scored on restarts play.

In the example we see a possible passage of play, with the white team scoring a goal with the help of an exterior neutral.

VARIATIONS

1. Touch limits.

2. Touch limits for the neutrals.

3. The players may enter the rectangle.

4. Vary the dimensions of the rectangle to adjust the difficulty level of the activity.

COACHING POINTS	<ul><li>Encourage the players to finish with a shot on goal as quickly as possible.</li><li>Play must be developed through the wings.</li><li>Encourage the players to look for the neutrals in order to create a numerical superiority.</li><li>The restricted zone leads the team in possession to widen their attacking front, which forces the opponent to open up their defense, which in turn creates wider spaces between the opponents.</li></ul>

6 VERSUS 6: RESTRICTED ZONE WITH EXTERIOR TEAMMATES

44

OPERATING METHOD Small-sided game

DURATION

14 minutes

OBJECTIVES

- Width
- Shooting on goal
- Defending the goal
- Switching play
- Possession

EQUIPMENT

- Cones to mark out the playing area
- Six bibs
- Two goals
- Balls

PREPARATION

Playing area: 25-35 x 35-45 meters.
Players: 14 + 2 goalkeepers.
Number of series: Two of 5 minutes with 2 minutes of recuperation between series.

ORGANIZATION

In the space chosen for the activity use the cones to set up the playing area. Set up a regulation size goal on each end line. In the middle of the field, set up a 10x8 meter rectangle. Divide the players into two teams of seven, who may move freely about the playing area, except for one player from each team who shall each be restricted to opposite sidelines. Two goalkeepers occupy their respective goals. One of the goalkeepers initiates play by passing to a teammate who will attack the opposite goal.

RULES

- The ball may not enter the central rectangle.
- When an interior player passes to an exterior player of the same color, the receiver carries the ball into the playing area, while the passer replaces them on the outside.
- When an interior player passes to an exterior player of a different color, the receiver only plays a supporting role and remains in their position.
- Each team attacks one goal and defends the other.
- Each goal scored is worth one point.
- Play is continuous. When a goal is scored, the goalkeeper of the team that was scored on restarts play.

In the example we see a possible passage of play, with the white team scoring a goal with the help of an exterior player.

VARIATIONS

1. Touch limits.

2. The players are also prohibited from entering the rectangle.

3. Vary the dimensions of the rectangle to adjust the difficulty level of the activity.

<table>
<tr><td>COACHING POINTS</td><td>

- Encourage the players to finish with a shot on goal as quickly as possible.
- Play must be developed through the wings.
- Encourage the defenders to defend all areas of the field.
- The restricted zone leads the team in possession to widen their attacking front, which forces the opponent to open up their defense, which in turn creates wider spaces between the opponents.

</td></tr>
</table>

6 VERSUS 6 WITH 2 NEUTRALS: MAN MARKING

45

OPERATING METHOD Small-sided game

DURATION

24 minutes

OBJECTIVES

- Marking
- Dismarking
- Possession

EQUIPMENT

- Five cones
- Eight bibs (six of one color and two of another)
- Two goals
- Balls

PREPARATION

Playing area: 40 x 50 meters.
Players: 14 + 2 goalkeepers.
Number of series: Two of 8 minutes with 4 minutes of recuperation between series.

ORGANIZATION

In one half of the field set up a 40x50 meter playing area with a goal on each end line. Divide the players into two teams of six, with 2 goalkeepers in their respective goals. Two neutrals in bibs of a different color are positioned within the playing area. One of the goalkeepers initiates play.

RULES

- All the players have a direct opponent to mark.
- The neutrals play with the team in possession.
- The neutrals may not score.

In the example we see a possible passage of play that ends with a goal for the white team.

VARIATIONS

1. The ball must stay on the ground.

2. The neutrals are restricted to two touches.

3. The neutrals may score.

COACHING POINTS	<ul><li>Train the reaction to the defensive transition: the player closest to where the ball is lost should press the opponent while the teammates reduce the space.</li><li>Train the collective spacing of the players.</li><li>Avoid having the players position themselves on the same line, in order to guarantee balance when combining.</li><li>Always provide the player in possession with at least two passing options.</li><li>If the player in possession is in a "free ball" situation, the players without the ball should attack space in a pre-set manner.</li></ul>

6 VERSUS 6 WITH 4 NEUTRALS: MAN MARKING

46

OPERATING METHOD Small-sided game

DURATION

24 minutes

OBJECTIVES

- Marking
- Dismarking
- Possession

EQUIPMENT	PREPARATION
<ul><li>Four cones</li><li>Ten bibs (six of one color and four of another)</li><li>Two goals</li><li>Balls</li></ul>	Playing area: 40 x 50 meters. Players: 16 + 2 goalkeepers. Number of series: Two of 8 minutes with 4 minutes of recuperation between series.

ORGANIZATION

In one half of the field set up a 40x50 meter playing area with a goal on each end line. Divide the players into two teams of six, with 2 goalkeepers in their respective goals. Two neutrals in bibs of a different color are positioned within the playing area, while two additional neutrals are positioned on the wings (one on each side). One of the goalkeepers initiates play.

RULES

- All the players have a direct opponent to mark.
- The neutrals play with the team in possession.
- The neutrals may not score.
- The neutrals may not pass to each other.

In the example we see a possible passage of play that ends with a goal for the white team.

VARIATIONS

1. The ball must stay on the ground.

2. The neutrals are restricted to three touches.

3. The neutrals may score.

4. Alternate the number of touches among the players: If one player plays with multiple touches and passes the ball, the next player must play with one touch. If the team maintains possession, the next player has unlimited touches.

<table>
<tr><td>COACHING POINTS</td><td>
<ul>
<li>Train the reaction to the defensive transition: the player closest to where the ball is lost should press the opponent while the teammates reduce the space.</li>
<li>Train the collective spacing of the players.</li>
<li>Avoid having the players position themselves on the same line, in order to guarantee balance when combining.</li>
<li>Always provide the player in possession with at least two passing options, especially options in support and to lay the ball off.</li>
<li>If the player in possession is in a "free ball" situation, the players without the ball should attack space in a pre-set manner.</li>
</ul>
</td></tr>
</table>

6 VERSUS 6 WITH 2 NEUTRALS AND 2 EXTERIOR TEAMMATES: MAN MARKING

47

OPERATING METHOD Small-sided game

DURATION

24 minutes

OBJECTIVES

- Marking
- Dismarking

EQUIPMENT	PREPARATION
<ul><li>Four cones</li><li>Nine bibs (seven of one color and two of another)</li><li>Two goals</li><li>Balls</li></ul>	Playing area: 40 x 50 meters. Players: 16 + 2 goalkeepers. Number of series: Two of 8 minutes with 4 minutes of recuperation between series.

ORGANIZATION

In one half of the field set up a 40x50 meter playing area with a goal on each end line. Divide the players into two teams of seven, with one player from each team positioned outside the playing area, on opposite sidelines. Two goalkeepers occupy their respective goals. Two neutrals in bibs of a different color are positioned within the playing area. One of the goalkeepers initiates play.

RULES

- All the players have a direct opponent to mark.
- The neutrals play with the team in possession.
- The neutrals may not score.
- The neutrals cannot pass the ball to each other.
- When an interior player passes to an exterior player of the same color, the receiver carries the ball into the playing area, while the passer replaces them on the outside.
- When an interior player passes to an exterior player of a different color, the receiver only plays a supporting role and remains in their position.

In the example we see a possible passage of play that ends with a goal for the white team.

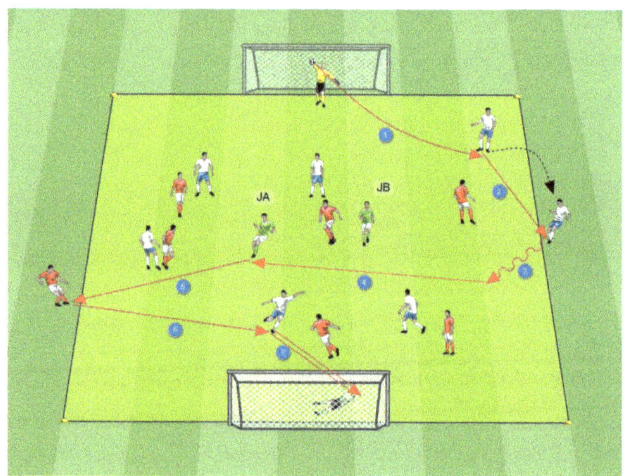

VARIATIONS

1. The ball must stay on the ground.

2. The neutrals are restricted to two touches.

3. The neutrals can score.

4. Alternate the number of touches among the players: If one player plays with multiple touches and passes the ball, the next player must play with one touch. If the team maintains possession, the next player has unlimited touches.

COACHING POINTS	<ul><li>Avoid having the players position themselves on the same line, in order to guarantee balance when combining.</li><li>Always provide the player in possession with at least two passing options.</li><li>If the player in possession is in a "free ball" situation, the players without the ball should attack space in a pre-set manner.</li></ul>

6 VERSUS 6 OCCUPYING THE ATTACKING ZONE

48

OPERATING METHOD Small-sided game

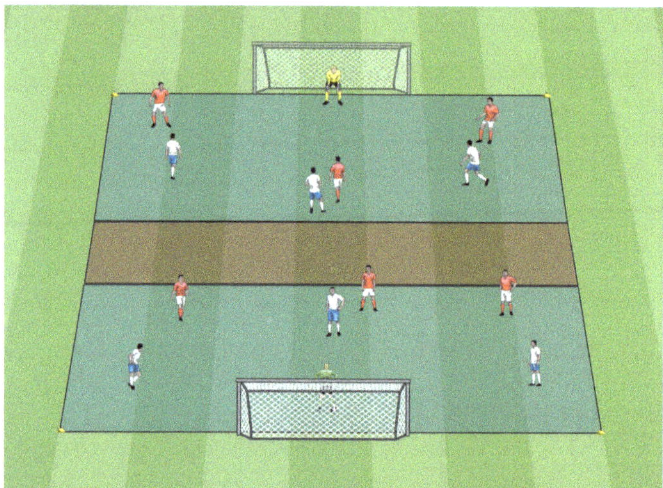

DURATION

24 minutes

OBJECTIVES

- Penetration
- Finishing
- Possession

EQUIPMENT	PREPARATION
<ul><li>Cones to mark out the playing area</li><li>Six bibs</li><li>Two goals</li><li>Balls</li></ul>	Playing area: 40 x 50 meters. Players: 12 + 2 goalkeepers. Number of series: Two of 8 minutes with 4 minutes of recuperation between series.

ORGANIZATION

In one half of the field set up a 40x50 meter playing area, with a central zone ten meters deep. Set up a goal on each end line. Divide the players into two teams of six, with two goalkeepers in their respective goals. One of the goalkeepers initiates play.

RULES

- Players cannot stop in the central zone.
- A goal is valid if, at the moment it is scored, all members of the team in possession are in the attacking zone.
- If there are any players (at least one) from the defending team in the central zone or their attacking zone at that time, the goal counts double.

In the example we see a possible passage of play that ends with a goal for the white team.

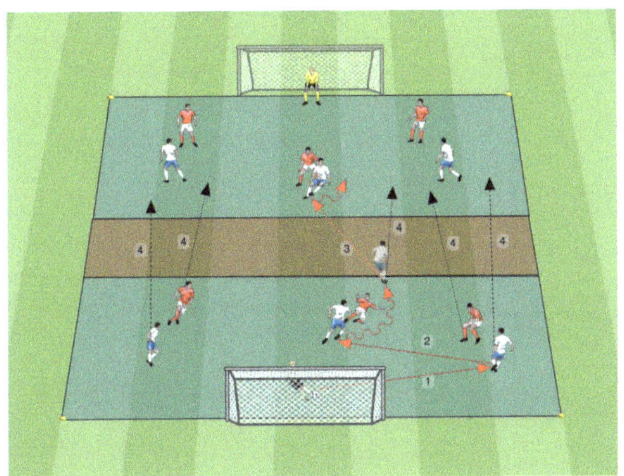

VARIATIONS

1. The ball must stay on the ground.

2. Alternate the number of touches among the players: If one player plays with multiple touches and passes the ball, the next player must play with one touch. If the team maintains possession, the next player has unlimited touches.

<table>
<tr>
<td>COACHING POINTS</td>
<td>

- Train the reaction to the defensive transition: the player closest to where the ball is lost should press the opponent while the teammates reduce the space.
- Train the collective spacing of the players.
- Avoid having the players position themselves on the same line, in order to guarantee balance when combining.
- Always provide the player in possession with at least two passing options, especially options in support and to lay the ball off.
- If the player in possession is in a "free ball" situation, the players without the ball should attack space in a pre-set manner.

</td>
</tr>
</table>

6 VERSUS 6 + 2 NEUTRALS: OCCUPYING THE ATTACKING ZONE

49

OPERATING METHOD Small-sided game

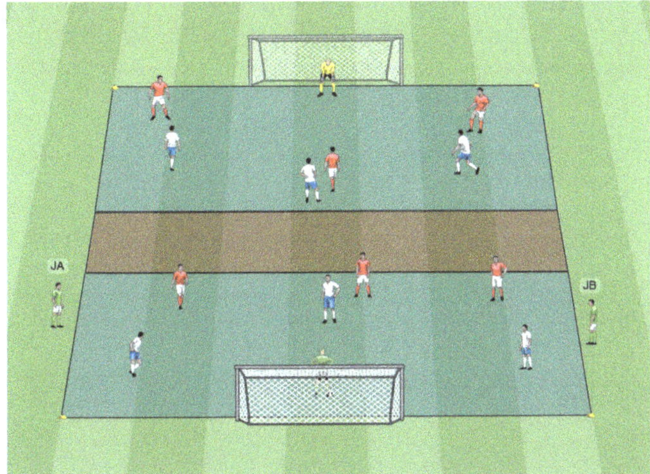

DURATION

24 minutes

OBJECTIVES

- Penetration
- Possession
- Passing
- Finishing

EQUIPMENT	PREPARATION

- Cones to mark out the playing area
- Eight bibs (six of one color and two of another)
- Two goals
- Balls

Playing area: 40 x 50 meters.
Players: 14 + 2 goalkeepers.
Number of series: Two of 8 minutes with 4 minutes of recuperation between series.

ORGANIZATION

In one half of the field set up a 40x50 meter playing area with a central zone ten meters deep. Set up a goal on each end line. Divide the players into two teams of six, with two goalkeepers in their respective goals and two neutrals (in bibs of a different color) positioned outside the playing area. One of the goalkeepers initiates play.

RULES

- Players cannot stop in the central zone.
- The neutrals play with the team in possession but are not allowed to dribble the ball.
- A goal is valid if, at the moment it is scored, all members of the team in possession are in the attacking zone.
- If there are any players (at least one) from the defending team in the central zone or their attacking zone at that time, the goal counts double.

In the example, we see a possible passage of play where the white team advances the ball into the attacking zone.

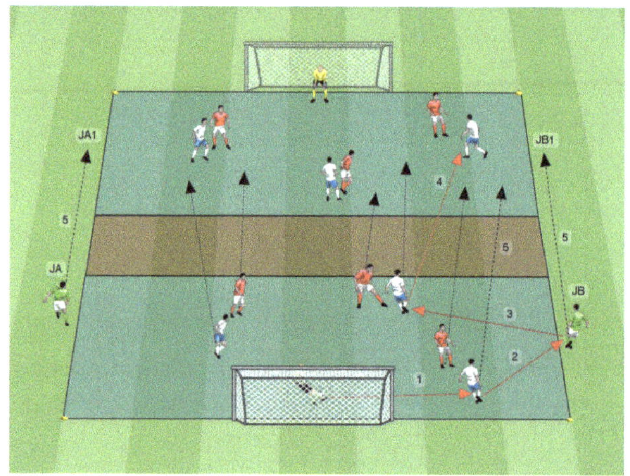

VARIATIONS

1. The ball must stay on the ground.

2. The neutrals play with a maximum of two touches.

3. The neutrals play with one touch.

4. Alternate the number of touches among the players: If one player plays with multiple touches and passes the ball, the next player must play with one touch. If the team maintains possession, the next player has unlimited touches.

COACHING POINTS	<ul><li>Train the reaction to the defensive transition: the player closest to where the ball is lost should press the opponent while the teammates reduce the space.</li><li>Avoid having the players position themselves on the same line, in order to guarantee balance when combining.</li><li>Always provide the player in possession with at least two passing options, especially options in support and to lay the ball off.</li><li>If the player in possession is in a "free ball" situation, the players without the ball should attack space in a pre-set manner.</li></ul>

6 VERSUS 6 + 2 EXTERIOR TEAMMATES: OCCUPYING THE ATTACKING ZONE

50

OPERATING METHOD Small-sided game

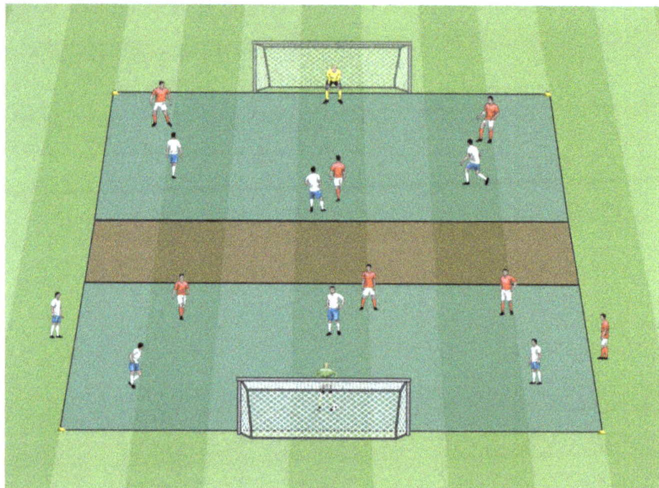

DURATION

24 minutes

OBJECTIVES

- Penetration
- Possession
- Passing
- Finishing

EQUIPMENT	PREPARATION
- Cones to mark out the playing area - Six bibs - Two goals - Balls	Playing area: 40 x 50 meters. Players: 14 + 2 goalkeepers. Number of series: Two of 8 minutes with 4 minutes of recuperation between series.

ORGANIZATION

In one half of the field set up a 40x50 meter playing area with a central zone ten meters deep. Set up a goal on each end line. Divide the players into two teams of seven, with one player from each team positioned outside the playing area, on opposite sidelines from each other. The two goalkeepers occupy their respective goals. One of the goalkeepers initiates play.

RULES

- Players cannot stop in the central zone.
- When an interior player passes to an exterior player of the same color, the receiver carries the ball into the playing area, while the passer replaces them on the outside.
- When an interior player passes to an exterior player of a different color, the receiver only plays a supporting role and remains in their position.
- A goal is valid if, at the moment it is scored, all members of the team in possession are in the attacking zone.
- If there are any players (at least one) from the defending team who are in the central zone or their attacking zone at that time, the goal counts double.

In the example, we see a possible passage of play that finishes with the players from the white team in the attacking zone.

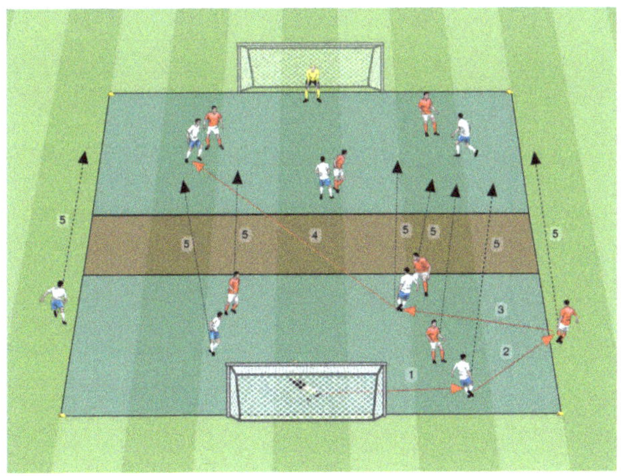

VARIATIONS

1. The ball must stay on the ground.

2. Alternate the number of touches among the players: If one player plays with multiple touches and passes the ball, the next player must play with one touch. If the team maintains possession, the next player has unlimited touches.

COACHING POINTS

- Train the reaction to the defensive transition: the player closest to where the ball is lost should press the opponent while the teammates reduce the space.
- Avoid having the players position themselves on the same line, in order to guarantee balance when combining.
- Always provide the player in possession with at least two passing options, especially options in support and to lay the ball off.
- If the player in possession is in a "free ball" situation, the players without the ball should attack space in a pre-set manner.

6 VERSUS 6 + 4 NEUTRALS PLAYING AERIAL BALLS

51

OPERATING METHOD	Small-sided game

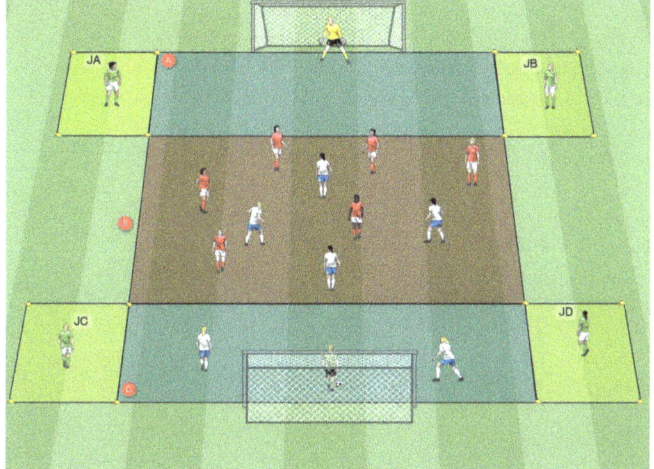

DURATION

24 minutes

OBJECTIVES

- Aerial balls
- Possession
- Shooting on goal
- Passing

EQUIPMENT

- **16 cones**
- **Ten bibs (six of one color and four of another)**
- **Two goals**
- **Balls**

PREPARATION

Playing area: 40 x 50 meters.
Players: 16 + 2 goalkeepers.
Number of series: Three of 5 minutes with 3 minutes of recuperation between each series.

ORGANIZATION

In one half of the field set up a 40x50 meter playing area with a zone 4 meters deep on each end (Zone A and Zone C). In each corner, set up a 4v4 meter square (as shown in the illustration), which will be the "aerial ball zones". Set up a regulation goal on each end line. Divide the players into two teams of six, with two goalkeepers occupying their respective goals. Arrange four players in bibs of a different colors in the aerial ball zones. One of the goalkeepers initiates play.

RULES

- Play starts from the goalkeeper, who passes the ball to their team.
- The four players in the aerial ball zones act as neutrals and play with the team in possession.
- Only the neutrals can enter the aerial ball zones.
- The neutrals play with a maximum of two touches.
- In zones A and C, a goal is only valid if it is scored with one touch or by an aerial finish.
- In Zone B (the central zone), the players can score in any manner.
- Change the neutrals after every series.

In the example we see a possible passage of play, with the forward of the white team scoring a headed goal after an aerial ball delivered from the right side (JB).

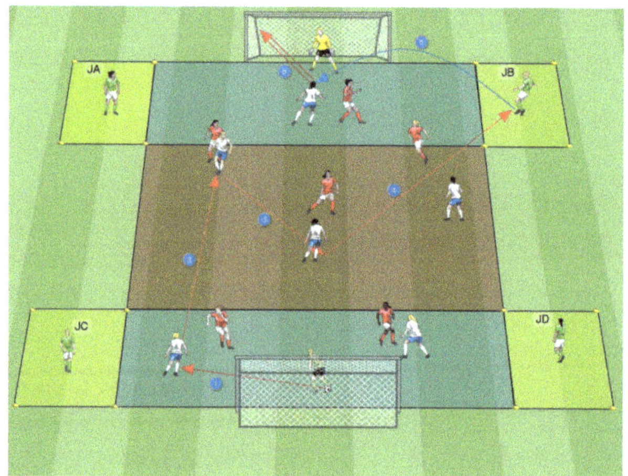

VARIATIONS

1. Require the teams to play on the ground except for the aerial services.

COACHING POINTS

- Train the reaction to the defensive transition: the player closest to where the ball is lost should press the opponent while the teammates reduce the space.
- Avoid having the players position themselves on the same line, in order to guarantee balance when combining.
- Always provide the player in possession with at least two passing options.
- If the player in possession is in a "free ball" situation, the players without the ball should attack space in a pre-set manner.
- After the player in possession releases the ball, they must move and make themselves available again.

6 VERSUS 6 WITH GOALKEEPERS AND 4 NEUTRALS WHO MAY ENTER THE PENALTY AREA

52

OPERATING METHOD Small-sided game

DURATION

24 minutes

OBJECTIVES

- Penetration
- Aerial balls
- Finishing

EQUIPMENT	PREPARATION
- 16 cones - 10 bibs (six of one color and four of another) - Two goals - Balls	Playing area: 40 x 50 meters. Players: 16 + 2 goalkeepers. Number of series: Three of 5 minutes with 3 minutes of recuperation between each series.

ORGANIZATION

In one half of the field set up a 40x50 meter playing area with a zone 4 meters deep on each end (Zone A and Zone C). In each corner, set up a 4v4 meter square (as shown in the illustration), which will be the "aerial ball zones". Set up a regulation goal on each end line. Divide the players into two teams of six, with two goalkeepers occupying their respective goals. Arrange four players in bibs of a different colors in the aerial ball zones. One of the goalkeepers initiates play.

RULES

- Play starts from the goalkeeper, who passes the ball to their team.
- The four players in the aerial ball zones act as neutrals and play with the team in possession.
- Only the neutrals can enter the aerial ball zones.
- The neutrals play with a maximum of two touches.
- In zones A and C, a goal is only valid if it is scored with one touch or by an aerial finish.
- In Zone B (the central zone), the players can score in any manner.
- When the aerial ball is delivered, the neutral on the opposite side may enter the penalty area and seek to finish. Afterwards, they must return to their square.
- Change the neutrals after every series.

In the example we see a possible passage of play, with the far side neutral player (JB) cutting into the penalty area and scoring a volley for the white team after an aerial ball delivered from the left side (JA).

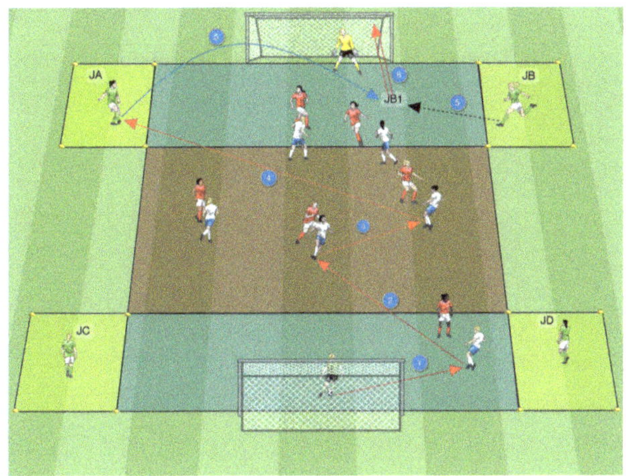

VARIATIONS

1. Require the teams to play on the ground except for the aerial services.

COACHING POINTS	<ul><li>Train the reaction to the defensive transition: the player closest to where the ball is lost should press the opponent while the teammates reduce the space.</li><li>Always provide the player in possession with at least two passing options.</li><li>If the player in possession is in a "free ball" situation, the players without the ball should attack space in a pre-set manner.</li><li>After the player in possession releases the ball, they must move and make themselves available again.</li></ul>

6 VERSUS 6 + 1 NEUTRAL: SCORE IN THE LARGE GOAL OR THE MINI-GOALS

53

OPERATING METHOD Small-sided game

DURATION

14 minutes

OBJECTIVES

- **Shooting on goal**
- **Defending the goal**
- **Switching play**

EQUIPMENT	PREPARATION
<ul><li>Cones to mark out the playing area</li><li>Seven bibs (six of one color and one of another)</li><li>Two goals</li><li>Eight tall cones</li><li>Balls</li></ul>	Playing area: 25-35 x 35-45 meters. Players: 13 + 2 goalkeepers. Number of series: Two of 5 minutes with 2 minutes of recuperation between series.

ORGANIZATION

In the space chosen for the activity set up a playing area with the cones. Set up a regulation size goal on each end line. In the four corners of the field, use the tall cones to set up four mini-goals, each about two meters wide. Divide the players into two teams of six (one is seen in white and the other in red bibs) who may move freely about the field. A neutral player (in a different color bib) also moves freely within the playing area. The two goalkeepers occupy their respective goals. One of the goalkeepers initiates play by passing to a teammate who will attack the opposite side.

RULES

- With the help of the neutral, the teams try to score in their opponent's large goal or mini-goals.
- A goal can only be scored in the regulation size goal with a header or a volley, while goals can be scored in the mini-goals in any manner.
- Goals scored in the regulation size goal count double.
- The neutral plays with the team in possession.

In the examples we see two possible passages of play: one ends with an aerial finish in the large goal for the white team after help from the neutral. In the other, the red team scores in the mini-goal after combining with the neutral.

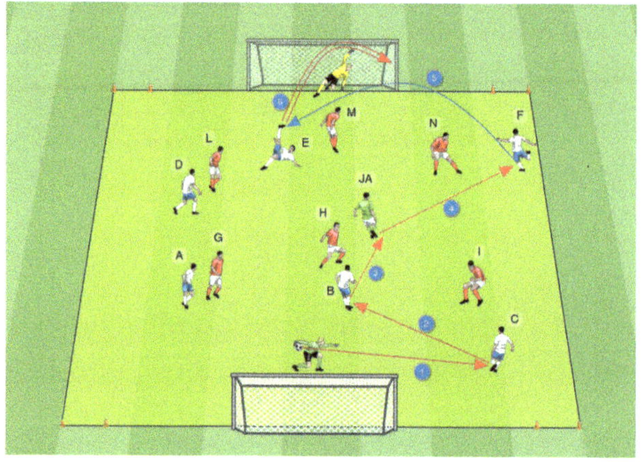

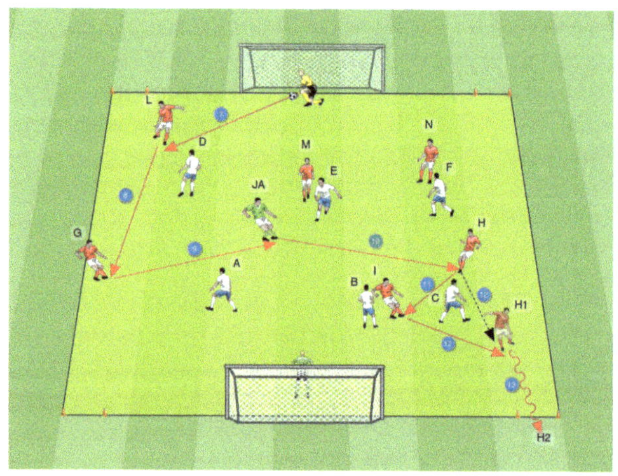

VARIATIONS

1. Touch limits.

2. Touch limits for the neutral.

3. Require interplay with the neutral or a pre-established number of passes before scoring a goal.

<table>
<tr><td>COACHING POINTS</td><td><ul><li>Encourage the attacking players to finish with a shot on goal as quickly as possible.</li><li>Encourage the attacking players to look for the easiest scoring option.</li><li>Encourage the defenders to move quickly to defend the three goals (the regulation size goal and the two mini-goals).</li><li>Encourage the attacking players to use the neutral player to take advantage of the numerical superiority.</li><li>Encourage the defenders to take up good positions to compensate for their numerical inferiority.</li></ul></td></tr>
</table>

5 VERSUS 5 + 2 NEUTRALS: SCORE IN THE LARGE GOAL OR THE MINI-GOALS

54

OPERATING METHOD Small-sided game

DURATION

14 minutes

OBJECTIVES

- Shooting on goal
- Defending the goal
- Switching play

EQUIPMENT

- Cones to mark out the playing area
- Eight bibs (six of one color and two of another)
- Two goals
- Eight tall cones
- Balls

PREPARATION

Playing area: 25-30 x 35-40 meters.
Players: 12 + 2 goalkeepers.
Number of series: Two of 5 minutes with 2 minutes of recuperation between series.

ORGANIZATION

In the space chosen for the activity use the cones to set up a playing area. Set up a regulation size goal on each end line. In the four corners of the field, use the tall cones to set up four mini-goals, each about two meters wide. Divide the players into two teams of five (one is seen in white and the other in red bibs) who may move freely about the field. The two neutral players (in bibs of a different color) operate outside the playing area; one on each side. The two goalkeepers occupy their respective goals. One of the goalkeepers initiates play by passing to a teammate who will attack the opposite side.

RULES

- A goal can only be scored in the regulation size goal with a header or a volley, while goals can be scored in the mini-goals in any manner.
- The neutrals operate outside the playing area and support the team in possession.
- The neutrals may not enter the playing area.
- The interior players may not leave the field to defend the neutrals.
- Goals scored in the regulation size goal count double.

In the example we can see two possible passages of play: one shows the white team scoring with a header in the large goal after combining with the two neutrals, the second shows a finish in one of the mini-goals by the red team, also scored with the help of the neutrals.

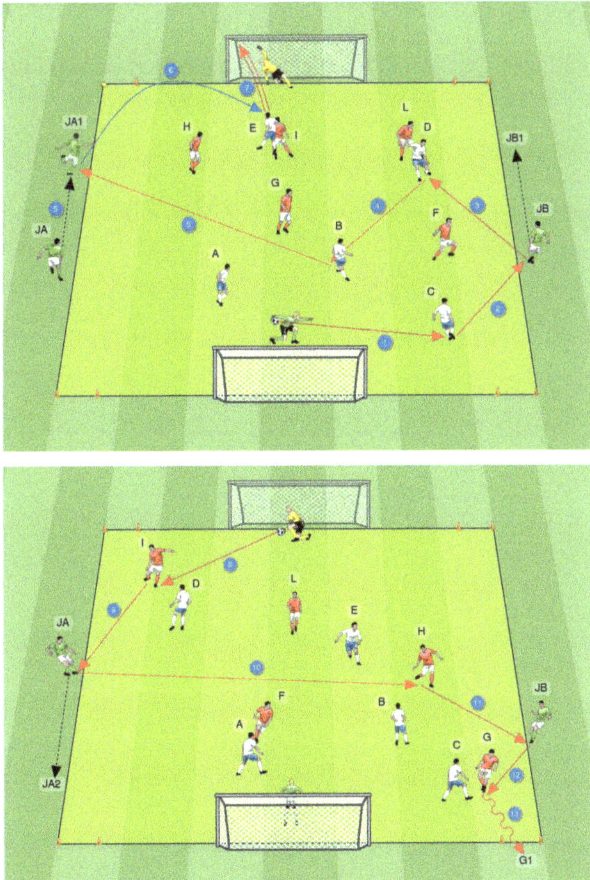

VARIATIONS

1. Touch limits.

2. Touch limits for the neutrals.

3. Require interplay with a neutral or a pre-established number of passes before scoring a goal.

COACHING POINTS	<ul><li>Encourage the attacking players to finish with a shot on goal as quickly as possible.</li><li>The initial numerical superiority facilitates rapid finishing.</li><li>In situations of momentary numerical inferiority, the defenders must mark the player with the ball and cover that player's teammates.</li><li>Avoid having the players position themselves on the same line, in order to guarantee balance when combining.</li><li>Always provide the player in possession with at least two passing options.</li></ul>

SITUATIONS OF MOMENTARY NUMERICAL SUPERIORITY

55

OPERATING METHOD Small-sided game

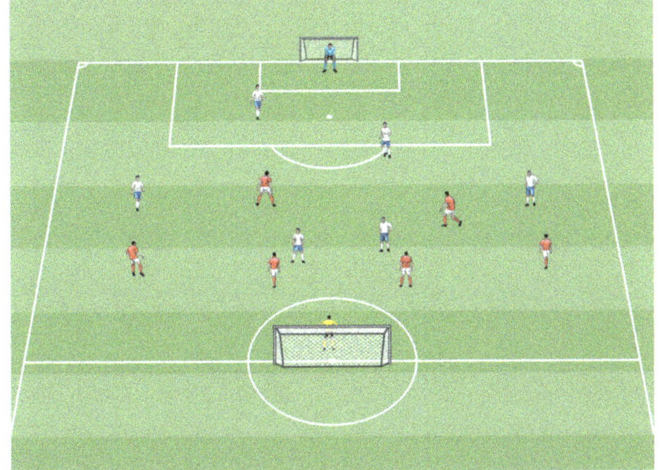

DURATION

14 minutes

OBJECTIVES

- Finishing
- Possession
- Aerobic capacity

EQUIPMENT	PREPARATION
<ul><li>Cones to set up the playing area</li><li>Six bibs</li><li>Two goals</li><li>Balls</li></ul>	Playing area: 55 x 50 meters. Players: 8/10/12 + 2 goalkeepers. Number of series: Two of 5 minutes with 2 minutes of recuperation between series.

ORGANIZATION

In the space chosen for the activity set up a playing area with the cones. Set up a goal on each end line. Divide the players into two teams of six (one team wearing bibs) who may move freely about the field. The two goalkeepers occupy their respective goals. One of the goalkeepers initiates play, passing to a teammate who will attack the opposite side.

RULES

- Each team attacks one goal and defends the other.
- Each goal scored is worth one point.
- When the ball is lost, whoever makes the mistake or gives up possession is momentarily eliminated from the game. That is; when someone loses the ball, they must run to the end line before rejoining the play.
- When the ball goes out of play, the goalkeeper restarts the game.
- The activity is continuous: if the ball leaves the playing area, restart play with the goalkeeper.

In the example we see a possible passage of play, with a player from the white team having to run to the end line after losing the ball.

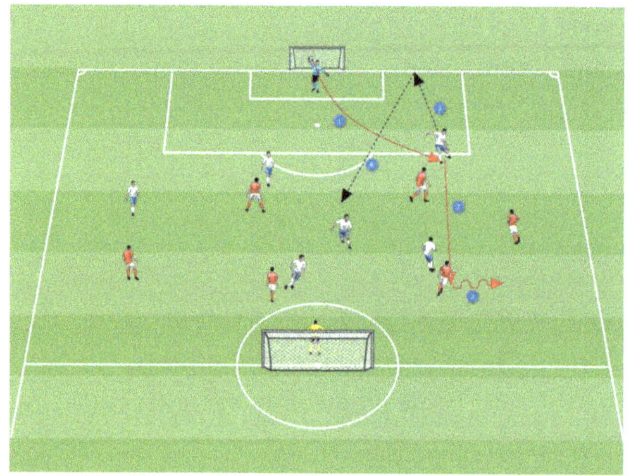

VARIATIONS

1. The player who passes to the player who loses the ball is momentarily eliminated from the game.

COACHING POINTS	<ul><li>Train the reaction to the defensive transition: the player closest to where the ball is lost should press the opponent while the teammates reduce the space.</li><li>Avoid having the players position themselves on the same line, in order to guarantee balance when combining.</li><li>Always provide the player in possession with at least two passing options.</li><li>Train body orientation when receiving the ball. The players need to be profiled to face as much of the field as possible.</li></ul>

GO TO THE END LINE BEFORE RETURNING TO THE GAME

56

OPERATING METHOD Small-sided game

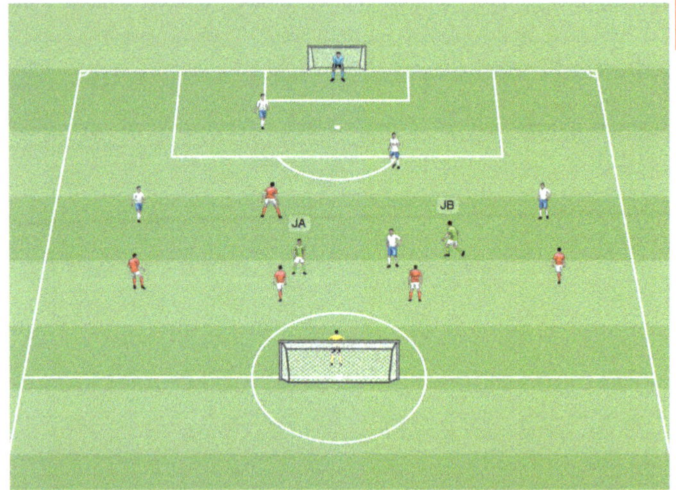

DURATION

14 minutes

OBJECTIVES

- Finishing
- Shooting on goal
- Defending the goal
- Possession

EQUIPMENT

- Cones to set up the playing area
- 7 bibs (five of one color and two of another)
- Two goals
- Balls

PREPARATION

Playing area: 55 x 50 meters.
Players: 8/10/12 + 2 goalkeepers.
Number of series: Two of 5 minutes with 2 minutes of recuperation between series.

ORGANIZATION

In the space chosen for the activity set up a playing area with the cones. Set up a goal on each end line. Divide the players into two teams of five (one team in bibs) who may move freely about the field. Two neutrals also operate within the playing area. The two goalkeepers occupy their respective goals. One of the goalkeepers initiates play by passing to a teammate who will attack the opposite side.

RULES

- Each team attacks one goal and defends the other.
- Each goal scored is worth one point.
- When the ball is lost, whoever makes the mistake or gives up possession is momentarily eliminated from the game. That is; when someone loses the ball, they must run to the end line before rejoining the play.
- When the ball goes out of play, the goalkeeper restarts the game.
- The two neutrals play with the team in possession, creating a situation of numerical superiority.
- The activity is continuous: if the ball leaves the playing area, restart play with the goalkeeper.

In the example we see a possible passage of play, with a player from the white team having to run to the end line after losing the ball.

VARIATIONS

1. Touch limits for the neutrals.

2. The player who passes to the player who loses the ball is momentarily eliminated from the game.

COACHING POINTS	<ul><li>Train the collective spacing of the players.</li><li>Avoid having the players position themselves on the same line, in order to guarantee balance when combining.</li><li>Train body orientation when receiving the ball. The players need to be profiled to face as much of the field as possible.</li></ul>

TEAM HANDBALL, SCORE WITH HEADERS

57

OPERATING METHOD Small-sided game

DURATION

20 minutes

OBJECTIVES

- Headers
- Defending the goal
- Finishing
- Warming up

EQUIPMENT	PREPARATION
<ul><li>Four tall cones</li><li>Eight small cones</li><li>Six bibs</li><li>Two goals</li><li>Balls</li></ul>	Playing area: 25-35 x 35-45 meters. Players: 8/10/12 + 2 goalkeepers. Number of series: Two of 6 minutes with 3 minutes of recuperation between series.

ORGANIZATION

In the space chosen for the activity set up a playing area with the cones. Set up a goal on each end line. Divide the players into two teams of six, with the goalkeepers occupying their respective goals. Play starts with one of the teams in possession.

RULES

- The teams can only pass the ball with their hands.
- Goals can only be scored by means of headers.
- If the ball hits the ground, the opposing team takes possession of the ball.

- The goalkeepers cannot leave their areas.
- Within the penalty area, the defenders may not intervene with their hands and may only head the ball.
- If the defenders use their hands in the penalty area, the opposing team is awarded a point.
- The teams may not make more than three passes with their hands.

In the example we see a possible passage of play that ends in a goal for the white team.

COACHING POINTS	- In possession: - Demand a staggering of the players that allows a balanced occupation of space. - Out of possession: - Demand high pressure in order to recover the ball as quickly as possible. - Balanced defending of the goal, according to collective tactical principles. - Players prepared for an attacking transition. - The goalkeeper gives verbal instructions to the defenders, and also takes up good positions in goal. - Encourage rapid vertical play when possible. - The players should have the ball in their hands as little as possible, instead favoring rapid interchanges when in possession.